Victoria Bennett

To Start The Year
From Its Quiet Centre

Indigo Dreams Publishing

First Edition: To Start The Year From Its Quiet Centre
First published in Great Britain in 2020 by:
Indigo Dreams Publishing
24, Forest Houses
Cookworthy Moor
Halwill
Beaworthy
Devon
EX21 5UU

www.indigodreams.co.uk

ISBN 978-1-912876-38-9

British Library Cataloguing in Publication Data. A CIP record for this book can be obtained from the British Library.

Designed and typeset in Palatino Linotype by Indigo Dreams.
Cover design from artwork by Jane Burn.
Printed and bound in Great Britain by 4edge Ltd.

Papers used by Indigo Dreams are recyclable products made from wood grown in sustainable forests following the guidance of the Forest Stewardship Council.

In memory of
Maureen Marie Bennett
1932 – 2015

"I lie here in a riot of sunlight
watching the day break and the clouds flying.
Everything is going to be all right."

~ Derek Mahon

Acknowledgements

To Adam and Django, thank you for always loving and believing me – you are the heart of my world.

Thanks also to Wendy Pratt, for her excellent guidance and mentorship in the process of writing and editing this pamphlet; Jason Weaver, for his patient proof-reading; Ruth, Gill and all the Wild Women, for being my creative tribe; my family, for showing me how to be strong; and finally, thank you to my mum, Maureen, who quietly made this world a kinder and more beautiful place to live.

The following poems have previously appeared:
Calendar — Highly Commended Charroux Memoir Prize 2019;
The Last Vigil (0.30am) — 'As Above So Below' online journal.

Also by Victoria Bennett:

Anchoring The Light
Fragile Bodies
Fragments
Byron Makes His Bed

CONTENTS

The Suede Shoes
after Thich Nhat Hanh

No good news from now
the doctor told us.
The nurse cried.
You did not.

I spend my days on the telephone,
searching for certainties:
names, dates, results,
chasing facts like dandelion wisps,
running out of time.

Sometimes, we talk about death.
Mostly, we talk about hospitals.
Bit by bit, their language claims us.

Meanwhile, the hen scratches
around the tree and the bees
collect nectar from a creeping vine.
The sun finally shines.

This is our in-between
living-and-dying time.

Why bother planting that seed?
Why turn the beds
for a summer that will never come?
Why bother buying the pretty suede shoes?

We choose the shoes because
we can still find joy in a step.
We plant the seed because
we still love the way
it insists itself into life.

We turn the beds because
there will always be a summer,
even after you are gone.

Soon, we shall have only echoes
but for now, we drink tea
and watch the clouds move,
watch the light pass
between the storm

and there is still good news.

When Did We Stop Bringing Flowers?

When April comes, I fill your room
with Black-Eyed Susan, sea-blue anemone.
By August, I add sunflowers, nasturtium,
flashes of orange against the window pane.
It makes sense to bring the garden inside,
so you can remember the beauty you made.
Looks like a florist on Fridays, you say.

As September drops its scattered leaves,
darkened mornings greet your medicated rise.
The offerings dwindle — one or two blooms.
October comes and with it the first frosts
but still I forage for sweet purple marjoram.
Even as November turns, I find something —
a twist of green mantle, a sprig of feverfew.

Your face turns away, cannot see.
You take hold of my hand, plead,
Why am I not dead?

So, no more cards.
No more florist store.
What are they for then,
the bright displays?

The New Nightdress

I rub your skin with oil of rose,
quietly masking the sweetness
of these dying days.

At night, I brush your weeping hair,
button the new nightdress,
fingers tender like a mother's,
tracing each lace flower.

> When she can no longer move,
> the doctor cuts it from her skin,
> frees her flesh from its hold.
> This garden has grown wild.

Calendar

Through my mother's window, days slip by,
moments so small we almost miss them
in our busy lives of dying:

the way the stocks begin to bend,
the first ash to fall, the lowering light.
Soon, the year will turn.

In the darkest days, she cries out
What time is it?
as if knowing can stop the clock.

She sleeps, wakes confused,
not sure if it has been minutes
or days that she's been gone.

In the morning, we greet the sun
with morphine and birdsong.
It's another beautiful dawn, I say

but they get harder.
Another one, she says,
eyes turning away.

The last one
and it is just me.
The rain begins.

Words For Dying To

How long have i got
        how will I know
                will you tell me
                        when the time comes

what is there
what will it be like

                I don't want to go

...I dreamt I was in an old church full of cobwebs and an old woman sat crouched in the corner all grey and fading and a young man came to her and held her hand and he sang and it was so beautiful it filled the church and I could feel the music inside me even though I woke up...I can still feel it now...the song...

what time is it
                it would be nice
                      if I could just go to sleep

I'm sorry I didn't write the letters

                        shall we go outside

...and I keep telling them it's not my legs...why have they got my legs tied...why won't they let me go...I want to go home...tell me what's going on...why has the blue straw-man come...I can't tell you...I mustn't be a fibbing-tibs or the nurse will be cross...

what time is it
                I thought I was dead
                  but maybe I'm not

is it morning or night
        have I been asleep

I did something silly last night
  I died and made myself come back

...Dad kept a look out for bombs you know...couldn't go to war...his heart...we hid in the Anderson...Ovaltine and malt sweets...damp on the walls...glad he never got to see how it all came to this...

it's getting too hard now
        I am very tired

                I think it's time to go

    I can't breathe
        my mouth is so dry

           what is happening

                who is here

I'm sorry
      I did it all wrong

I don't recommend this to anyone

                do not touch.

Broken

The paramedic tells me
he must remove
the wedding band.

I hear the pliers snap.

You search for your husband,
who cups the broken circle in his hands,
whispers *hush...*

          I close the door quietly.
          There is nothing more to do.

The Last Vigil

10.30pm   The nurse asks me again
if this is what I want to do.

She won't feel it anymore.

I watch mute
as the drugs drive
into the port.

Bonnie Lass, get some sleep.

11.45pm   The hospice nurse talks about
her grandson, how hard it is
to know what to give
an eight-year-old boy.

Upstairs, my own son sleeps,
dreams of morning,
the first advent window,
Santa Claus and secret surprises.

I know the signs. I have read them
in the cancer-care books,
midnight-Googled them online
and yet, I cannot find the words.

I stand to leave the room, knowing
you will not go until I do.
At the door, I pause and turn
to say goodnight, just once more.

I reach the fourth step of the stairs
before the nurse calls; my feet jumping
three at a time, like a child hurrying
to catch a glimpse before you disappear.

0.15am Brown foam bubbles from your mouth.
I wipe it away, just like you did
when I was a child, your finger
wrapped in a rough handkerchief.

When the others arrive they ask
is she…? I tell them
there is still time to say goodbye
even though it is a lie.

I move aside,
finally letting go.

0.30am After it all, three small breaths —

so quiet,
I almost missed you leaving.

You travel upwards,

weightless,
turning cartwheels —

why did no-one tell me
death felt like this —

an unbearable joy?

You leap from star
to star and then,

you are gone.

The quiet of the dark,
faint night-singing.

December Hovers On The Advent Hour

My sister and I watch the empty trees.
Across the moon, the night clouds run.
I am sure I hear you laughing, riding
the back of the storm, all the way.

How To Watch Someone Die

First, let go of all the plans
you once had: the casual ways
we assume the right to live.
Create a box for all your future tense.
Catch yesterdays in your upturned hands,
unfurl memories, learn to read code.
Before long, these too will be dust.

Abandon sleep. Forget the clock
and roll like a wave
on dawns and dusks that drip
like morphine into days
that feel as if they could go
on and on and on, but never
look away, in case you miss
the moment that it ends.

Learn to live between the punctuated hours,
your ears attuned like the city fox
to spot an altered breath,
your eyes alert to the pallor of skin.

Juggle everything, and fail,
and tell yourself this is your best
and know this best will never be enough.
Accept you cannot change any of this,
and break, and get back up again.

Try not to let them die before they die,
try to let them stay in this world
even as this world gets smaller
every day, even if some days
you wish an end to this
and when it comes

try to remember
to stop, to sit
and listen

to the silence
after
the dying is done;

watch the morning come.

Try all over again
to let go,
and live.

Post Mortem

My mother's heart weighed
three hundred and twenty-eight grams.
It doesn't seem enough.

Her lungs weighed seven hundred and forty-seven grams
on the right, one thousand, four hundred and nineteen
on the left: a bag and a half of tumour in each breath.

Her kidneys were one hundred and seventeen grams
and clean to the end. Her spleen, an abstract organ,
came in a close second at one hundred and sixteen.

Her brain recorded one thousand, two hundred
and fifteen grams: a fair weight for a life
of memories with nowhere now to go.

On final count, she weighed seventy-five kilograms.
The rest was cancer, thirty-two kilos drained away.
Which is good. She never wanted to be fat

but it doesn't seem right that her heart
weighed so much less than her death.
It carried so much through all the years.

She died saying she had no regrets.
Maybe that is what made it so light:

all the spent stuff left behind
so she could pass easy to the other side.

Polypharmacy

I do not want to give them back.
The names like a litany:
      Zomorph, Dexamethasone,
        Gabapentin, Lorazepam,
          Oramorph, Omeprazole.
All those punctuated days and nights,
the rise and fall of pain;
the prayer calls of cancer.

These boxes are all I have left.
They are my map back
to the beginning of death.

Doses and numbers spreading like paths
until we reach the last vials:
      Morphine,
        Midazolam,
          Cyclizine.
Clear liquids that take her away,
render her mute, her eyes closed,
searching for the lost child.
What is happening to me?

Her last words:
Do Not Touch.

I hate them all, these drugs
that took her, piece by piece
and yet, my hands linger.
This was what I gave her:

a year of days without schisms of pain,
without sickness and then,
when the screaming came,
an end, something like peace.

I do not want to let go but I do,
the unspoken words left hanging
as they take them away:

my mother is dead.

Even so, I wake in the night,
my clock still set to her needs,
a reflex reach for the medicine box.
Come on, Mum, please?

My hand returning empty in the dark.

Tell Me Lies

Please, do not tell me of your perfect deaths.
Do not speak of surrounding light,
slipping serenely out of sight.

Please, do not tell me of your perfect goodbyes.
Tell me nothing or tell me lies.
In turn, I will tell you mine:

that the drugs do work,
that the pain is short,
that once the oxygen stops,

the heart will start to give.

Planting

After your death,
I dig bulbs into your bones:

bluebells, daffodils,
snake's-head fritillaries.

They are my prayers
for your safe passing.

The Almanac tells me
I am too late.

Even so, I wait, patient,
for the flowers to show.

Solway
after Neruda

Today, I can write of this heaviness;
the way damp mist-nets hang
over every breath,
swallowing the words.

It takes them all
until there is only air,
ghost-like through the leaves.

There is Always More To Lose

The voice goes first:
intonations, familiar words,
unexpectedly silent.

Soon too, the body leaves.
The way it moves,
the texture of touch

but the face is always here.
It catches me in windows
as I walk along the street,

whispers — *stop,*
you are forgetting me.
At night, as I sleep

it wraps itself around
my mouth, threads silver
through my hair.

After The War, The Battle Comes

Those who walk away
travel as time-travellers do,
slightly out of synch, somewhere
between the living and the dead.
Wounds heal but the shadows
are stitched in. It takes time
to learn to move in this strange skin.

October

I long for the changing light,
the curl of mist on the ash tree,
the quiet hush towards winter.
I want to remember this time;

the mornings as they rise,
waiting for the midpoint
where the blue shines through
to roll back the day.

To watch the way leaves fall,
the garden returning to still;
the bones of summer
silhouetted against the sky.

Strange to say, these quiet days
where our end was marked
by the rounding of the dark,
these were the best of days.

Our time slowed
to the smallness of things;
the closing bud,
the bee's last flight.

Cooking

Somewhere between the carrots
and the leeks, my legs buckle.

A sound bubbles up,
forms into a single word:
mum-mum-mum-mum
and here I am, small and scared,
reaching for a hand that isn't there,
her face turned out to the distance,
her back closed.

I bang my fists on the floor,
begging her to come back.

Between the longing
and fury, I gulp at the air,
drop the knife to the floor
and begin to crawl
out of the door
and up the stairs
    — hand-knee-hand-knee —
all the time stuttering
mum-mum-mum-mum.

I open the wardrobe,
pull out the drawer,
spray Lily-of-the-Valley
into the air. It reeks
of synthetic flowers,
rubbing alcohol, and underneath

a cloying, sweeter smell
— a mix of piss
and blood and death —
the smell of decay.

I take the embroidered pillow,
raise it to my face
and breathe her in.

I unfold the red cotton bag
that held her pills,
start to recite the names,
falter,
and find I have forgotten some.
How can that be?

I reach deeper, pull out
the answerphone,
plug it in and press *Play*.

Message after message.
Her voice.

Hello…hello…
  are you there?
    I guess you are too busy…
      Darling, are you there?
       Hello…
        Hello?
         Pick up the phone, love…
          It's me.

I'm here, Mum.
Come home

St Bees, November

I fold the softness of stones around my palms,
fill pockets with cold catchers of dreams.
This is the beach of my father's childhood.

When my mother dies, an old friend writes
to tell me how she'd loved him
as if there was no other in the world.

I have come here to discover them again:
the iron-haired boy and the raven-curled girl.
On the rocks, I find their two names carved.

Maureen and Walter, 1949

I trace my fingertips along the stretch of time.
The names are fading. I can sense them drifting.
This is what our death is to be,

softly erasing our place in things,
returning us to the space of sound and mist,
where the sky meets silver land

and the tides are not full of sorrow
but stones, singing:
a story yet to be told.

Postcard Home

I travel the world in small steps,
find myself in places you would have loved.
Out on the silver shore, walking braced against the wind,
I can see you, your red coat picked out in all this blue.
Here you are now, walking up to the little white house,
salt-blasted, happy. I like to think of you here,
living by the sea at last, your paints out beside you,
brushes dipped in ink as the day closes.
I like to think of you this free, but still,
I miss you being here with me.

To Start The Year From Its Quiet Centre

It is enough
to feel
the pebble roll
in my hand,

to curl, cat-like,
warm in the sun,
into an hour
of not doing,

to stand, long enough
to hear the curlew call;
to remember our lives
opening to it all.

Indigo Dreams Publishing Ltd
24, Forest Houses
Cookworthy Moor
Halwill
Beaworthy
Devon
EX21 5UU
www.indigodreams.co.uk

MASTER THE FREE MIND

*Reset Your Brain, Control Your Thoughts and
Unlock the Power of Your Subconscious Mind*

Gabriel O. Daniels

TABLE OF CONTENTS

INTRODUCTION

In our modern, hyper-connected world, we are constantly flooded with external stimuli competing for our attention and mental resources. Our minds are persistently overwhelmed by social media, news, work, and the demands of everyday life, leaving us little opportunity to truly connect with our inner selves. As we continuously relinquish our mental capacities to these distractions, we inadvertently limit our ability to unlock our full human potential. The problem we face is not solely the overpowering influence of external factors but also our inability to recognize and take control of our minds. We have become increasingly dependent on external validation and instant gratification, losing sight of our inherent power to shape our lives, futures, and, ultimately, our destinies. This disconnection from our inner selves and the surrender of control to outside forces impede our capacity to reach our highest potential.

This book aims to guide you on a transformative journey that will empower you to master your mind, reset your brain, and reclaim the control you have unwittingly surrendered. Combining scientific research, practical techniques, and powerful insights, you will learn to break free from the constraints of external stimuli and forge a new path towards personal growth, fulfillment, and self-actualization. By understanding and addressing the root causes of your disempowerment, you can begin to cultivate unshakable inner strength, resilience, and clarity of purpose that will propel us towards our greatest potential.

To achieve this transformation, we will delve into the following topics: the brain and its parts, providing a comprehensive understanding of its structure and function; breaking habits, with practical strategies to reshape and replace unproductive patterns; epigenetics, exploring the dynamic relationship between our genes and the environment; neuroplasticity, revealing the brain's remarkable capacity for adaptation and change; the placebo effect, examining its powerful impact on our perceptions and healing processes; brainwaves, understanding their significance in our mental and emotional states; the science of meditation, uncovering its profound effects on health, well-being, and consciousness; coherence, exploring the concept of harmony and balance in our lives; and finally, a deepened exploration of quantum reality and its role in shaping our experiences and perceptions. Through these interconnected topics, you will gain a comprehensive understanding of the intricate relationships between your brain, your consciousness, and the reality you inhabit. With this knowledge, you will be equipped with the tools and insights necessary to actively create the life you desire, tapping into your limitless potential for growth, fulfillment, and self-actualization. By mastering your mind and taking control of your reality, you can unlock the door to a world of endless possibilities and infinite potential.

My lifelong passion for understanding the conscious and unconscious aspects of the human mind has driven me to explore the depths of our mental landscape. I firmly believe that living life to the fullest potential is a key aspect of a purposeful existence, and I have dedicated my life to the pursuit of knowledge and personal growth. My adventurous life experiences have taken me across the globe, living and working in various countries and immersing myself in diverse cultures, environments, races, social classes, and ages. Throughout my journey, I have been fortunate enough to encounter remarkable mentors, healers, scientists and coaches who have shared their wisdom and provided opportunities for continued learning. These experiences have led me to participate in seminars, host meetings, and events, and engage in numerous pursuits to further my understanding of the human mind. Navigating through this rich tapestry of cultural and personal interactions demanded the highest form of self-discipline, consistent problem-solving skills, and calmness in high-stress situations. I have developed an adaptable and growth-oriented mindset that has allowed me to thrive in the face of constant change. Each encounter, challenge, and success has served me well in deepening my comprehension of the mind's complexities and potential. By leveraging this unique background and the wisdom gained from these experiences, I am better equipped to help others in their quest for personal growth, self-empowerment, and realizing their fullest potential.

In this book, I share the invaluable lessons I have learned from my own experiences, the teachings of my mentors, and my ongoing exploration of the human mind. Drawing on this wealth of knowledge and experience, I will provide you with a comprehensive guide to mastering your mind, resetting your brain, and reaching your full human potential. Embark on this journey of self-empowerment and growth, and begin living a more purposeful and fulfilling life. This book is designed to empower you to regain control of your mind and provide tangible benefits that will significantly enhance your quality of life. By investing your time and energy into understanding the strategies and techniques outlined in this book, you can expect to experience a range of positive outcomes.

As you delve deeper into the workings of your mind, you will gain heightened self-awareness, allowing you to recognize your thought patterns, emotions, and behaviors. This understanding will enable you to identify your strengths and weaknesses, make better decisions, and align your actions with your goals and values. Additionally, by learning to filter out external distractions and hone in on what truly matters, you will develop greater mental clarity and focus, boosting your productivity and overall performance in both your personal and professional life. Mastering your mind and developing a growth-oriented mindset will also help you become more resilient in the face of adversity and better equipped to adapt to change. This resilience will enable you to bounce back from setbacks and embrace new opportunities, leading to a more fulfilling and successful life. Moreover, you will cultivate greater emotional intelligence by understanding and managing your own emotions and empathizing with the emotions of others, which will improve your relationships and enhance your overall well-being. You will develop a stronger sense of purpose as you reconnect with your inner self and discover your passions, values, and goals. This clarity will provide you with the motivation and drive to pursue your dreams and positively impact the world around you. Finally, mastering your mind and cultivating a more balanced, centered, and grounded mental state will lead to a deep sense of inner peace and happiness. This inner tranquility will radiate throughout your life, resulting in more harmonious relationships and greater fulfillment.

My passion for understanding the human mind and my personal growth journey have inspired me to share my knowledge and experience with others. Over the years, I have been successfully coaching individuals to develop a similar mindset, empowering them to unlock their full potential and experience the myriad benefits of mastering the mind and resetting the brain. Through my coaching practice, I have witnessed incredible transformations in the lives of my clients. They have experienced heightened self-awareness, enabling them to make better decisions and align their actions with their goals and values. They have also developed mental clarity and focus, leading to increased productivity and effectiveness in their personal and professional lives. Witnessing these transformations in my clients' lives has been humbling and inspiring. Their successes reaffirmed my belief in mastering the mind to unlock one's full human potential. As a result, I have been compelled to share this knowledge and these strategies with a broader audience through this book. In writing this book, I will guide you on your transformative journey, empowering you to experience the same profound benefits. By applying the principles outlined in this book, you can unlock your full human potential and experience the myriad benefits of mastering your mind and resetting your brain.

I promise that as you diligently apply and internalize the principles and insights presented in this book, you will inevitably experience significant transformations in your life. By embracing the knowledge and strategies shared here, you will naturally shift your thoughts, behaviors, and habits, aligning your actions with your desired outcomes. In doing so, you will break free from the constraints of your old self and pave the way for the reinvention of a new, empowered version of yourself, fully equipped to reach your full potential and live the life you've always envisioned. Time is our most precious and finite resource, and there is no better moment to embark on this transformative journey than now. With so much more to gain than to lose, every piece of knowledge acquired through this book will help you map out your place in relation to your reality and bring you closer to living a life that serves your greatest purpose. The longer you wait to take control of your mind and unleash your innate capabilities, the more opportunities for growth and fulfillment you may miss. Take the first step towards change before another day passes. Seize this opportunity and make a commitment to yourself today. Invest in your personal growth, and harness the power of your mind to create the life you've always desired. The journey towards a better, more purposeful life begins with a single step—take that step now, and embrace the incredible transformation that awaits you. Remember, you have everything to gain and nothing to lose; each insight will contribute to the rich tapestry of your life, leading you towards a future filled with purpose, passion, and boundless potential.

THE BRAIN
Chapter One

THE BRAIN'S CORE FUNCTIONS AND THE POWER OF THE CENTRAL NERVOUS SYSTEM

Prepare to explore the brain - that miraculous and complex organ in human anatomy! It makes you who you are and is responsible for your thoughts, emotions, and experiences. The brain is the ultimate multitasker, working tirelessly every day to keep you alive and functioning. It's responsible for crucial bodily functions like breathing and heartbeat and more intricate ones like analyzing complex problems and creating creative ideas. The human brain is a complex and intricate organ that serves as the command center of our body, responsible for controlling our thoughts, emotions, and actions. The brain cannot do everything by itself; it needs help from the central nervous system. This network of nerves, comprising the brain and spinal cord, receives and processes all sensory information. Imagine the central nervous system as an orchestra conductor, receiving information from all the instruments (sensory organs) and creating a harmonious response. The peripheral nervous system gathers information from the body's sensory organs and sends it to the central nervous system for processing. It's like sending a message to the brain, which then decides how to respond. The central nervous system sends signals to the motor nerves, which allow the body to move and respond to external stimuli.

The brain is composed of billions of neurons, which are specialized cells that communicate with one another through electrochemical signals. These neurons form intricate networks, allowing for the efficient transmission of information throughout the brain and body. With its diverse responsibilities, the brain plays a crucial role in maintaining our daily functions, regulating our responses to stimuli, and even shaping our personalities. It is essential to explore its various components, their individual functions, and how they interact with one another to facilitate our thoughts, actions, and experiences.

The brain's primary functions can be broadly categorized into several key areas, including processing sensory information, coordinating motor functions, regulating homeostasis, facilitating learning and memory, and governing higher cognitive functions such as reasoning, problem-solving, and decision-making. Our sensory organs, including our eyes, ears, nose, tongue, and skin, work tirelessly to collect a wealth of information about our surroundings. This information is then sent to the brain through intricate networks of neural pathways. Upon receiving this sensory data, the brain processes and integrates the information, allowing us to perceive and comprehend the world around us. Each sensory system plays a unique role in delivering specific information to the brain. For instance, our visual system is responsible for processing light, color, and movement information, which helps us recognize objects, discern colors, and detect motion. This complex process begins when light enters the eye and is absorbed by specialized cells called photoreceptors. These cells convert light into electrical signals, which are then sent to the brain via the optic nerve. Once in the brain, these signals are processed by various regions, ultimately allowing us to perceive and interpret visual information. Similarly, our auditory system processes sound and helps us locate the sources of those sounds. This process starts when sound waves enter the ear and cause vibrations in the eardrum, which then transfers these vibrations to the inner ear structures. Hair cells in the inner ear convert the vibrations into electrical impulses that travel along the auditory nerve to the brain. Different brain regions are responsible for processing the various aspects of sound, such as pitch, volume, and direction. By integrating this information, our brain can recognize and interpret the sounds we hear and determine their origin.

The olfactory system detects and identifies various odor molecules in our environment. This process begins in the nasal cavity, where specialized olfactory receptor neurons are located. When odor molecules enter the nose, they bind to these receptors, triggering an electrical signal that travels to the olfactory bulb, a region in the brain responsible for processing smell. The olfactory bulb then sends this information to other brain regions, including the limbic system, which is involved in emotion and memory. This connection helps explain why certain smells can evoke strong emotions and memories. The gustatory system allows us to perceive and differentiate between various tastes, such as sweet, salty, sour, bitter, and umami (savory). This process starts when we consume food or drink, which comes into contact with our taste buds, small sensory organs located on the tongue, and other regions of the mouth. Each taste bud contains specialized taste receptor cells, which detect specific taste molecules and transmit this information to the brain. The taste-related signals travel via the gustatory nerve to the gustatory cortex, a region in the brain that processes and interprets taste information. The gustatory system works closely with the olfactory system, as flavor is a combination of both taste and smell.

The somatosensory system processes a wide range of tactile sensations, including pressure, vibration, temperature, pain, and proprioception (awareness of body position and movement). This system relies on various specialized sensory receptors in the skin, muscles, joints, and other tissues. These receptors detect specific stimuli and convert them into electrical impulses that are transmitted to the brain via the spinal cord. The signals are then processed by the somatosensory cortex, a region in the brain that interprets and integrates tactile information. The somatosensory system plays a vital role in our daily lives, allowing us to perceive and respond to our physical environment, avoid injury, and maintain balance and coordination.

The brain plays a crucial part in controlling and coordinating both voluntary and involuntary movements within our bodies. The initiation of motor commands takes place in the motor cortex, a specialized region within the cerebral cortex. These commands are then relayed to the spinal cord and the peripheral nerves, which activate our muscles, allowing us to move. The spinal cord is an integral part of the central nervous system and connects the brain to the rest of the body, allowing communication between the two. It's like a superhighway ensuring messages are sent quickly and efficiently. It also serves as a reflex center, which means it can initiate automatic responses to sensory input without the need for conscious thought. Imagine your hand moving away from a hot stove before your brain realizes what's happening.

A central role of the brain is regulating various aspects of homeostasis, such as body temperature, blood pressure, and hormone levels, ensuring that these factors remain within a balanced and healthy range. Homeostasis is a vital physiological function that allows our bodies to maintain a stable internal environment, enabling us to operate optimally despite external fluctuations. The hypothalamus (Figure 1), a small but essential region located at the base of the brain, is a key player in maintaining homeostasis. This area is responsible for receiving and integrating information from many sensory inputs, such as temperature receptors and blood-borne signals, which help monitor the body's internal conditions. After processing this information, the hypothalamus sends signals to other regions of the brain, as well as to various organs and systems throughout the body. These signals trigger adjustments and adaptations that work to maintain a balanced internal state, ensuring our bodies remain stable and function efficiently. For example, suppose our body temperature rises above its normal range. In that case, the hypothalamus will activate mechanisms to cool us down, such as initiating sweating or dilating blood vessels near the skin's surface. Conversely, if our body temperature drops too low, the hypothalamus will stimulate processes to conserve and generate heat, such as shivering or constricting blood vessels to reduce heat loss. In this way, the brain, specifically the hypothalamus, plays a crucial role in maintaining homeostasis, allowing us to adapt to a constantly changing environment and ensuring our bodies remain balanced for optimal functioning.

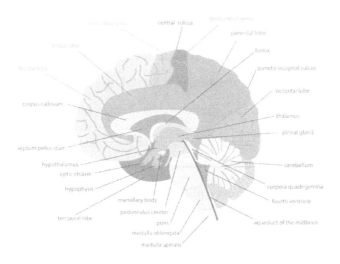

Figure 1: The brain in all its parts.

One of the brain's most remarkable abilities is its ability to learn from our experiences and store memories, allowing us to navigate our lives effectively and adapt to new situations. This essential function is facilitated by several brain regions and complex neural networks, with the hippocampus playing a central role in the process. The hippocampus, a critical structure within the limbic system, is heavily involved in consolidating new information and transforming it into long-term memories. This process occurs as we encounter new experiences, acquire new skills, or gather new knowledge. The hippocampus helps organize and stabilize these memories, ensuring they are encoded and stored for future retrieval. In addition to the hippocampus, various other neural networks and pathways in the brain contribute to the storage and retrieval of memories. For example, the prefrontal cortex is involved in working memory, which allows us to hold and manipulate information in our minds for short periods. The amygdala, another limbic system structure, is crucial for processing and encoding emotional memories, particularly those related to fear and threat. When we need to recall past experiences or access stored memories, these interconnected neural networks work together to retrieve the relevant information. This retrieval process enables us to use our memories to inform our present decisions and actions, providing valuable guidance based on our previous experiences. For instance, we might recall a past mistake and use the memory of that experience to avoid making the same error again.

In addition to these primary functions, the brain is also

responsible for a range of higher cognitive processes that underpin our ability to think, reason, and make decisions. The cerebral cortex (Figure 2) is the brain's outermost layer, which plays a crucial role in our higher cognitive functions, such as perception, reasoning, decision-making, and memory. This thin, wrinkled layer of gray matter is composed of billions of neurons, and its intricate folding allows for a larger surface area to be packed into the limited space of the skull. The cerebral cortex is divided into four primary lobes, each responsible for specific aspects of brain function. The frontal lobes are the largest and most complex of the four lobes located at the front of the brain. They are responsible for various cognitive functions, such as planning, problem-solving, decision-making, and controlling voluntary movements. The prefrontal cortex, part of the frontal lobes, plays a crucial role in personality, social behavior, and emotional regulation. Additionally, Broca's area, located in the left frontal lobe, is responsible for speech production and language comprehension. Situated behind the frontal lobes and above the temporal lobes, the parietal lobes are primarily responsible for processing bodily sensory information, such as touch, temperature, and pain. The primary somatosensory cortex, located in the parietal lobes, receives and processes sensory input from the skin, muscles, and joints, allowing us to perceive and interpret various sensations. The parietal lobes are also involved in spatial awareness and coordination, enabling us to interact with our environment effectively.

The temporal lobes are located on either side of the brain,

beneath the parietal and frontal lobes. They are primarily responsible for processing auditory information and are involved in memory formation, language comprehension, and emotion regulation. The primary auditory cortex, located in the temporal lobes, receives and processes sound input from the ears. Located at the back of the brain, the occipital lobes are primarily responsible for processing visual information. The primary visual cortex, situated in the occipital lobes, receives and processes visual input from the eyes, allowing us to perceive and interpret the world around us. The occipital lobes also involve optical recognition, enabling us to identify objects, faces, and colors.

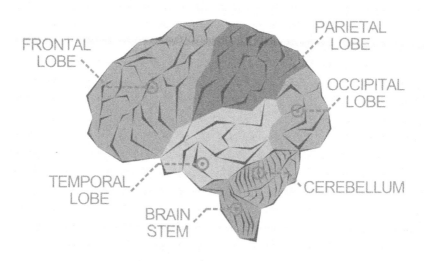

Figure 2: The Cerebral Cortex.

The cerebral cortex, its lobes, and the limbic system play

critical roles in our cognitive abilities and higher brain functions, contributing to processes such as perception, memory, decision-making, and emotional regulation. Each lobe is responsible for specific functions, working together to create a seamless and integrated experience of the world. Understanding the roles of these lobes can provide valuable insight into the complex workings of the human brain, which ultimately shapes our thoughts, actions, and experiences. It is often referred to as the brain's emotional center, playing a crucial role in forming emotional memories and regulating various physiological functions. The key components of the limbic system (Figure 3) include the amygdala, hippocampus, thalamus, hypothalamus, and cingulate gyrus. Each of these structures contributes to the overall functioning of the limbic system, allowing us to experience and navigate the emotional aspects of our lives.

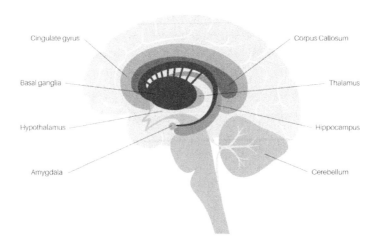

Figure 3: The Limbic System.

Located deep within the temporal lobes, the amygdala is an almond-shaped structure primarily responsible for processing emotions, particularly fear and anxiety. It receives sensory input from various regions of the brain and is responsible for coordinating emotional responses to stimuli. The amygdala also plays a role in emotional memory, enabling us to recall emotionally charged events more vividly than neutral events. Situated adjacent to the amygdala, the hippocampus is a seahorse-shaped structure responsible for forming and consolidating new memories. It converts short-term memories into long-term memories, allowing us to retain information over extended periods. The hippocampus is also involved in spatial memory and navigation, enabling us to remember and navigate our environment effectively. The thalamus is a paired structure located deep within the brain, functioning as a relay station for sensory information. It receives input from various sensory organs, such as the eyes, ears, and skin, and forwards the information to the appropriate regions of the cerebral cortex for further processing. The thalamus also plays a role in regulating arousal and consciousness, as well as the sleep-wake cycle. Located below the thalamus, the hypothalamus is a small but essential structure responsible for maintaining the body's internal balance or homeostasis. It regulates various physiological functions, such as body temperature, hunger, thirst, and sleep, as well as controlling the release of hormones through its connection with the pituitary gland. The hypothalamus also plays a role in emotional regulation, linking the limbic system to the autonomic nervous, and endocrine systems.

The cingulate gyrus is a curved structure above the corpus callosum, the bundle of nerve fibers connecting the brain's two hemispheres. It involves various cognitive and emotional processes, such as attention, motivation, and empathy. The cingulate gyrus also contributes to the regulation of emotional responses and the formation of emotional memories. The various structures within the limbic system work together to process and regulate our emotional experiences, helping to shape our thoughts and actions. Think of the limbic system as the emotional core of your brain. It determines whether you feel happy or sad, angry or calm, and stores memories that shape personality and worldview. Understanding the role of the limbic system can provide valuable insights into the complex interplay between emotions and cognitive processes, shedding light on the intricacies of human behavior and experience.

The pineal gland and pituitary gland are two essential glands in the brain that support the limbic system and perform independent functions in the brain and body. The pineal gland is a small endocrine gland located deep within the brain, specifically in the epithalamus, and is responsible for producing and secreting the hormone melatonin. Melatonin is a hormone that regulates sleep and wake cycles and balances the body's circadian rhythms. The pineal gland is connected to the visual system and responds to light and dark changes, which helps regulate the body's natural sleep-wake cycle. Additionally, the pineal gland has been suggested to play a role in modulating mood, enhancing immune function, and regulating the reproductive system. In some spiritual and esoteric traditions, the pineal gland is considered the "third eye" or the "seat of the soul." It is believed to be a point of inner vision and intuition, where higher states of consciousness and spiritual awareness can be accessed.

The pituitary gland is often called the "master gland" because it controls the function of many other endocrine glands in the body. The pituitary gland is divided into the anterior pituitary and the posterior pituitary. The anterior pituitary produces and secretes several hormones that regulate growth, metabolism, reproduction, and stress response. These hormones include growth hormone, thyroid-stimulating hormone, follicle-stimulating hormone, luteinizing hormone, and adrenocorticotropic hormone, among others. The posterior pituitary releases two hormones, oxytocin, and vasopressin, which regulate water balance, blood pressure, and social behavior. While the limbic system focuses on the emotional and cognitive aspects of our lives, the brainstem attends to the fundamental physiological processes that keep us alive and functioning. Both of these complex structures work in harmony to shape our experiences and ensure the proper functioning of our bodies and minds.

Consider your brainstem like the body's autopilot system, ensuring all essential functions run flawlessly even when you're not paying attention. It also regulates our sleep-wake cycle, digestion, and other critical functions. Located at the base of the brain and connected to the spinal cord, the brainstem is comprised of three main parts: the midbrain, the pons, and the medulla oblongata. These components work together to control various automatic processes, including respiration, heart rate, blood pressure, digestion, reflexes, and other vital functions. The midbrain, also known as the mesencephalon, is the uppermost section of the brainstem. It is involved in several vital functions, including regulating eye movements, auditory and visual processing, and coordination of motor movements. The midbrain contains the substantia nigra, a crucial structure in the production of dopamine, a neurotransmitter responsible for the control of voluntary movement and the regulation of reward and motivation. The pons below the midbrain serve as a relay center for information passing between the cerebrum, cerebellum, and spinal cord. It is essential for regulating sleep, respiration, and facial movements. The pons also plays a role in the modulation of pain signals and controls bladder function. The medulla oblongata is the lowest part of the brainstem, positioned between the pons and the spinal cord. It controls some of the most critical automatic functions, such as heart rate, blood pressure, and respiration. The medulla also regulates reflexes like coughing, swallowing, and vomiting, as well as coordinating the actions of the digestive system. In addition to maintaining vital physiological functions, the brainstem also serves as a conduit for nerve signals traveling between the brain and the rest of the body. The brainstem contains several cranial nerve nuclei that transmit sensory and motor information to and from the head and neck. These nerve nuclei regulate facial expressions, taste, hearing, and balance functions.

The brain is an extraordinary and intricate organ that serves as the command center for our body, regulating our thoughts, emotions, and actions. As we explore the intricacies of the brain and its various components, we gain a deeper understanding of the processes that shape our experiences, personalities, and lives. The human brain is a marvel of nature, and it is through our ongoing exploration that we can appreciate the incredible capacity of this vital organ.

THE DYNAMIC INTERPLAY OF THOUGHTS, ACTIONS AND EXPERIENCES

Neurotransmitters can be thought of as the postal service of the brain, playing a pivotal role in transmitting messages between nerve cells, or neurons, in the brain and the rest of the nervous system. These signaling molecules influence various functions, from muscle contractions and organ functions to our thoughts, emotions, and behavior. The brain's storytelling process shapes these thoughts and emotions, which creates narratives based on the information it receives. For example, suppose you've had a negative experience with public speaking. In that case, your brain may create a story that you're not good at it, leading to anxiety and avoidance when faced with public speaking opportunities. Neurotransmitters are synthesized and stored in tiny sacs called vesicles within the neurons and are released into the synaptic cleft, the gap between two neurons, upon receiving a signal. Once released, they bind to specific receptors on the receiving neuron, initiating a response or inhibiting an action.

However, the brain's influence doesn't stop at our thoughts and emotions - it also impacts our behavior. Think of the brain as a puppet master, pulling the strings that determine our actions and reactions. Our behavior is influenced by various factors, including genetics, environment, and past experiences - all of which are processed and analyzed by the brain. Numerous critical neurotransmitters influence our mood and behavior, some of the most prominent being serotonin, dopamine, norepinephrine, and gamma-aminobutyric acid (GABA). Each neurotransmitter plays a unique role in the brain and nervous system, affecting various aspects of our thoughts, emotions, and actions. Imbalances in the levels of these neurotransmitters have been linked to various mental health disorders and can lead to alterations in mood, motivation, and overall psychological well-being.

Serotonin, often called the "feel-good" neurotransmitter, plays a crucial role in regulating mood, appetite, sleep, and health. It is primarily synthesized in the brain and gastrointestinal tract, and its levels can significantly impact our mental and physical health. For example, low serotonin levels have been linked to depression, anxiety, and sleep disorders, while healthy levels contribute to feelings of happiness and contentment. Imagine a person who is experiencing a period of high stress, such as starting a new job or moving to a new city. This individual may experience a decrease in serotonin levels due to the pressure, which in turn can lead to feelings of anxiety, irritability, and difficulty sleeping. However, this person can alleviate some of these symptoms and improve their overall mood by engaging in activities that boost serotonin levels, such as exercise, exposure to natural sunlight, or maintaining a balanced diet. This shows how an individual's serotonin levels can significantly impact their daily life and demonstrates the importance of understanding the role of neurotransmitters in modulating mood and behavior.

Dopamine is a crucial neurotransmitter in the brain, often associated with feelings of pleasure and reward. It plays a significant role in regulating motivation, decision-making, and the reinforcement of certain behaviors. When we engage in activities that we find enjoyable or rewarding, such as eating a delicious meal, exercising, or achieving a personal goal, our brain releases dopamine, reinforcing the positive feelings associated with these experiences. Imagine a student who has been studying diligently for an important exam. When they receive their test results and see that they've achieved a high score, their brain releases a surge of dopamine. This release creates a sense of pleasure and satisfaction, reinforcing the idea that their hard work and effort have paid off. As a result, the student becomes more motivated to continue studying and working hard in the future, as they associate these actions with the rewarding sensation of dopamine release. However, dopamine imbalances can also lead to issues such as addiction or compulsive behaviors, as individuals may seek out activities or substances that artificially stimulate the release of dopamine. Compulsive behaviors such as excessive gambling, overeating, drug abuse, or even excessive use of social media can also be driven by the pursuit of pleasurable sensations associated with increased dopamine levels. This imbalance can create a cycle of dependence, as the individual craves pleasurable sensations, and over time, their brain may become less responsive to natural dopamine release. As a result, the person may require higher doses or more intense experiences to achieve the same level of pleasure, further perpetuating the cycle and making it increasingly difficult to break free from the grasp of addiction or compulsive behavior.

Norepinephrine, or noradrenaline, is another vital neurotransmitter in the brain that significantly regulates our mood, attention, and stress response. It functions as a neurotransmitter and a hormone, affecting various brain and body parts. Norepinephrine is involved in the "fight or flight" response, helping to increase our alertness and prepare our bodies to respond to perceived threats or challenges. Picture a person walking through a dark alley late at night. They suddenly hear footsteps rapidly approaching from behind, causing their brain to release norepinephrine. This release triggers the "fight or flight" response, increasing their heart rate, blood pressure, and blood flow to the muscles, making them more alert and ready to react to the potential danger. In addition to its role in the stress response, norepinephrine also influences other cognitive functions such as attention, focus, and memory. However, imbalances in norepinephrine levels can contribute to various mental health conditions, such as anxiety, depression, and attention deficit hyperactivity disorder (ADHD).

Gamma-aminobutyric acid (GABA) is a crucial inhibitory neurotransmitter in the central nervous system, playing a vital role in regulating our mood, anxiety levels, and overall sense of calm. By inhibiting or reducing certain neurons' activity, GABA helps maintain a healthy balance between neuronal excitation and inhibition, allowing our brains to function optimally and promoting a sense of relaxation. To better understand the role of GABA, imagine preparing for an important job interview. As the interview approaches, you might feel a surge of anxiety and nervousness. In response, your brain releases GABA, which acts as a natural calming agent, helping to reduce excessive neuronal activity and allowing you to regain composure and focus during the interview. GABA is also involved in other aspects of brain function, such as muscle control, sleep regulation, and the reduction of inflammation. A deficiency in GABA levels can lead to various symptoms, including anxiety, insomnia, and even certain seizure disorders.

Understanding the role of neurotransmitters in mood and behavior can provide valuable insights into the neurobiological underpinnings of various psychological disorders and pave the way for the development of more effective treatments. By studying the complex interactions between these chemical messengers and the brain's intricate network of neurons, researchers can continue to unravel the mysteries of human emotions, behavior, and mental health. The role of the brain in perception and decision-making is fundamental to our understanding of the world around us and our ability to navigate through it effectively. Perception is the process by which our brains receive, interpret, and make sense of sensory information from our environment. Decision-making, on the other hand, involves the evaluation of available options and the selection of an appropriate course of action. Both processes are complex and involve the interaction of multiple brain regions and neural circuits. Neurotransmitters and their influence on mood and behavior are just one piece of the puzzle when it comes to understanding the complexity of the human brain. Another equally important aspect is how the brain processes sensory information and makes decisions based on that input. Perception begins when sensory information from our environment, such as light, sound, or touch, is collected by specialized receptor cells and transmitted to the brain. The information then undergoes a series of transformations as it is processed by various brain regions. A key brain region involved in decision-making is the prefrontal cortex, responsible for executive functions such as planning, reasoning, and impulse control. The prefrontal cortex helps to evaluate available options, weigh their potential consequences, and ultimately select a course of action based on our priorities and values. One illustrative example of perception and decision-making in action is the process of crossing a busy street. Our brains must first perceive the visual and auditory information from the environment, such as the positions and speeds of oncoming vehicles and the sounds of engines and horns. This information is processed and integrated with our knowledge of traffic rules and past experiences to determine the appropriate moment to cross safely. The prefrontal cortex then evaluates the potential risks and benefits of crossing and decides to either wait or proceed.

Emotions can influence decision-making by affecting how we evaluate options and biasing our choices towards those that promise greater rewards or reduced risks. This intricate interplay between perception, decision-making, and emotions makes it clear that our mental processes are not isolated but deeply intertwined, ultimately guiding our actions and shaping our experiences. Building on the influence of emotions in perception and decision-making, it is essential to consider cognitive biases, which are systematic patterns of deviation from rationality in judgment that often lead to perceptual distortion, inaccurate judgment, or illogical interpretation of information. They impact our mind, mental health, and body by shaping our thoughts, emotions, and behaviors.

Anchoring Bias

Anchoring bias is the tendency to rely heavily on the first piece of information encountered when making decisions. This initial information, or "anchor," influences our judgment, even if it is not necessarily accurate or reliable. Consider a person negotiating the price of a car. If the seller initially quotes a price of $30,000 and then lowers it to $20,000, the buyer may perceive this as a great deal, influenced by the initial anchor of $30,000. However, the buyer may view it as an unfavorable deal if the seller quotes $10,000 and raises it to $20,000. In both cases, the anchoring bias has affected the buyer's perception of the deal, regardless of the car's actual value.

Availability Heuristic Bias

This bias occurs when people overestimate the importance of information that is readily available to them. It can lead to distorted judgments and perceptions of reality, as individuals place too much weight on information that is easily recalled or accessed. Some people may perceive terrorism as the biggest threat to their country due to its frequent coverage in the media. However, this perception may not accurately reflect the reality of the situation, as other less-publicized dangers may pose greater risks. The availability heuristic bias can contribute to irrational fears and influence our decision-making processes.

Bandwagon Effect

The bandwagon effect describes the tendency for people to adopt certain beliefs or behaviors simply because others are doing so. This can lead to conformity and groupthink, stifling creativity and innovation. An individual might vote for a popular political candidate because others are doing so, rather than critically evaluating the candidate's qualifications and policy positions. In the workplace, the bandwagon effect can hinder diverse perspectives and limit the potential for innovative solutions.

Choice-Supportive Bias

Choice-supportive bias occurs when people defend their decisions or choices, regardless of their merit or accuracy, simply because they made them. This bias can lead to a distorted perception of reality and hinder our ability to learn from our mistakes. Someone who purchases an iPhone might focus on its positive aspects and downplay the advantages of a Samsung Galaxy. This bias can manifest in various aspects of life, such as defending one's chosen political candidate or justifying a decision to adopt a particular lifestyle.

Confirmation Bias

Confirmation bias refers to the tendency to search for, interpret, and remember information in a way that confirms our pre-existing beliefs. This bias can lead to a narrow-minded approach to problem-solving and decision-making, as we may disregard or dismiss conflicting evidence. A person who believes that apple seeds are unhealthy may seek out articles and videos that support this belief while ignoring the evidence suggesting that apple seeds might have some benefits when consumed in moderation. In scientific research, confirmation bias can result in flawed conclusions and hinder the advancement of knowledge.

Ostrich Bias

The ostrich bias refers to our subconscious decision to ignore negative information and focus on the positive aspects of a situation. This bias goes beyond simply looking for positive information; it involves actively ignoring negative information even when it is readily available. Imagine you have an assignment that you don't want to do. Instead of completing the task, you procrastinate, hoping the problem will go away on its own. Similarly, smokers often ignore the negative health implications of cigarettes, thinking they will not be affected by the consequences. This bias can lead to a lack of personal growth, as it promotes ignorance and prevents us from addressing our problems head-on.

Outcome Bias

Outcome bias is a cognitive bias that occurs when we judge the quality of a decision based on the outcome it produces rather than the quality of the decision-making process itself. For example, a student might cram for a test at the last minute and happen to do well, leading them to believe that procrastination is an effective study strategy. However, this success might have been due to luck, and the student could have achieved even better results if they had studied more effectively. Focusing only on the outcome can lead to poor decision-making, as it fails to consider the conditions and factors that existed at the time of the decision.

Overconfidence Bias

Overconfidence bias is when we become overly confident in our abilities and decisions, often due to a series of past successes. For example, a stock trader who has made several profitable trades may start to believe that any stock they pick will be successful, even without thoroughly researching their choices. This dangerous mindset can lead to a lack of critical thinking and an overreliance on one's opinions, potentially resulting in significant losses. It is crucial to remain grounded and continue to base decisions on facts and evidence rather than relying solely on past success.

Survivorship Bias

Survivorship bias occurs when we judge a situation or phenomenon based on the information that has survived rather than considering all the relevant data. For example, articles claiming that performing certain tasks every morning will make you a millionaire often overlook the many people who followed the same routine but did not achieve the same level of success. This bias can lead to unrealistic expectations and an inaccurate understanding of what it takes to succeed. It is essential to consider all available data rather than focusing solely on the most successful cases when making decisions or evaluating a situation.

Selective Perception

Selective perception is a cognitive bias that causes people to perceive messages and actions according to their frame of reference. As a result, individuals tend to overlook and forget information that contradicts their beliefs or expectations. Imagine you are a smoker and a big fan of soccer. You are more likely to notice advertisements about soccer because you have a positive perception of the sport. Conversely, you may ignore negative cigarette advertisements, as you have already accepted smoking as a part of your life. This bias demonstrates how our subconscious mind filters information, leading us to focus on what aligns with our existing beliefs and preferences.

Blind Spot Bias

Blind spot bias refers to our tendency to believe we are less biased than others. We often perceive ourselves as objective and rational, basing our judgments on facts and statistics. However, this belief can make us oblivious to our own biases. Suppose you give a gift to your teacher, and she subsequently gives you a good grade on a test. If you ask her whether she was biased when grading your paper, she may genuinely believe that the gift did not influence her decision. However, if you ask her if other teachers might be biased when students give them gifts, she is likely to say yes in most cases.

These biases can distort our perception of reality, hinder personal growth, and negatively impact our decision-making processes. By cultivating self-awareness, seeking diverse perspectives, practicing empathy, and being open to feedback, we can actively work to counteract the influence of cognitive biases. The brain's influence over our experiences is also significant. It acts like a filter, shaping how we perceive and interpret the world. Our perceptions and emotions are colored by what goes on inside of us - all shaped by that same storytelling process in the brain. By becoming aware of the brain's influence, we can work to shape our thoughts and behaviors positively. We can learn to recognize and challenge negative narratives, replacing them with more helpful ones. We can also work to rewire our brains by intentionally engaging in positive behaviors and experiences, leading to new neural pathways and positive changes in behavior and outlook.

HABITS
Chapter Two

IDENTIFYING HABITS AND PATTERNS

In today's fast-paced and constantly changing world, the ability to adapt and evolve is more important than ever. Our habits, behaviors, and thought patterns shape how we experience life, influence our relationships, and determine our overall well-being. While some of these habits may serve us well, others can hold us back, preventing us from reaching our full potential. It is within our power to break free from the chains of old habits and patterns and to embrace a new and improved version of ourselves. This transformation starts with understanding the nature of our habits, identifying the ones that no longer serve us, and replacing them with more positive and empowering alternatives.

The journey to personal transformation begins with recognizing and understanding the negative habits and patterns that hold us back from achieving our full potential. These habits manifest as repeated behaviors or thought processes that hinder our personal growth, compromise our physical or mental health, and adversely affect our relationships or various aspects of our lives. Gaining insight into the nature of these patterns is essential for breaking their hold on our lives and embarking on a path towards greater fulfillment and self-improvement. To fully understand the effects of your negative habits and patterns, it is necessary to analyze their consequences on various aspects of your life. This process involves considering both the immediate and long-term repercussions of these behaviors.

Start by examining the short-term consequences of your negative habits. For instance, how do these behaviors affect your mood, energy levels, and ability to focus or perform tasks? Are they causing you to feel stressed, anxious, or overwhelmed? Do they lead to impulsive decisions or actions that you later regret? Reflecting on these immediate effects will provide insight into how your negative habits hinder your daily functioning. Next, consider the long-term consequences of your negative patterns. How have these behaviors impacted your physical health over time? Are they contributing to chronic health issues, sleep disturbances, or weight gain? Additionally, evaluate the effect of your habits on your mental health. Are they perpetuating feelings of guilt, shame, or low self-esteem? Have they led to more serious mental health issues such as depression or anxiety disorders? Furthermore, assess the impact of your negative habits on your relationships with others. Are they causing conflicts, misunderstandings, or feelings of isolation? Do they prevent you from forming deep connections or maintaining healthy relationships with loved ones? Also, consider how your negative habits and patterns affect your work performance and career goals. Are they hindering your productivity, stifling your creativity, or causing you to miss out on opportunities for growth and advancement? Finally, reflect on the overall impact of these behaviors on your life satisfaction. Are they preventing you from achieving your goals or living a fulfilling and meaningful life? Are they causing a general sense of unhappiness or discontentment?

By understanding the negative impact of your habits and patterns on various aspects of your life, you'll be better equipped to find the motivation and commitment required to change them. Gaining this comprehensive perspective will highlight the urgency of addressing these behaviors and help you identify areas where you can implement changes to improve your overall well-being and life satisfaction. This awareness is a crucial step in breaking the cycle of negative habits and working towards a healthier, happier version of yourself. As you develop greater self-awareness and recognize your negative habits and patterns, creating a comprehensive list of these behaviors is essential. This list will provide you with a clear and organized overview of the areas in your life that need improvement. Be as specific as possible when noting down each habit or pattern, including the context in which they typically occur and the emotions or triggers associated with them.

This list will be a valuable tool for guiding your growth journey. It will not only help you stay focused on your goals but also allow you to track your progress as you work on each habit or pattern. Regularly reviewing and updating your list can be an excellent way to maintain motivation and celebrate your achievements, no matter how small they may seem. Consider organizing your list by categorizing habits and patterns based on their impact on your life or the level of difficulty in addressing them. You can prioritize tackling the most detrimental habits first or start with the ones that seem easier to change, gradually building your confidence and momentum for more significant transformations. Having a clear and structured list of your negative habits and patterns will help you develop a more focused and effective plan for overcoming them. It will also serve as a visual reminder of your commitment to personal growth and the progress you make along the way. To facilitate self-reflection and help identify negative habits that may hinder personal growth, it is beneficial to examine a list of common habits many individuals struggle with:

Procrastination

Procrastination, the act of habitually delaying or postponing tasks and decisions, is a pervasive issue that can significantly impact various aspects of an individual's life. Often seen as a harmless tendency to put things off, procrastination can have far-reaching consequences on a person's mental and emotional well-being, work performance, and interpersonal relationships. Chronic procrastination can create a vicious cycle of self-defeating behavior, undermining self-esteem and hindering personal and professional growth. By understanding the complexities of procrastination and recognizing its impact on our lives, we can take the necessary steps to overcome this barrier and unlock our full potential. As we gain a deeper understanding of the complexities of procrastination, it is essential to acknowledge the different factors contributing to this behavior. Factors such as fear of failure, perfectionism, and poor time management can all play a role in fostering a habit of procrastination. By addressing these underlying causes, individuals can begin to take control of their lives and break free from the constraints of chronic procrastination. Overcoming procrastination is an important aspect of personal growth and can be achieved by implementing several key strategies. These include developing methods to manage time more effectively and setting realistic goals for oneself. By focusing on these areas, individuals can enhance their productivity, minimize the negative effects of procrastination, and make significant progress towards achieving their objectives.

Negative Self-Talk

Negative self-talk can profoundly impact various aspects of an individual's life, including motivation, self-sabotage, and overall life satisfaction. When individuals consistently engage in self-critical thoughts and pessimistic inner dialogue, they create an environment where negativity thrives, and personal growth is stifled. Negative self-talk often reinforces the belief that one is incapable or undeserving of success. As a result, individuals may feel demotivated and less likely to pursue their goals or take advantage of opportunities that come their way. Internalizing these negative beliefs limits their potential for growth and the possibility of achieving their aspirations. Constant negative self-talk can lead to pervasive dissatisfaction with oneself and one's life. Individuals may struggle to recognize or appreciate their strengths and accomplishments by focusing on perceived flaws and failures. This distorted self-perception can create a sense of unhappiness and discontent, negatively impacting mental health, and life satisfaction.

Overthinking

Another habit that can be limiting is overthinking, which involves excessive analyzing, evaluating, and dwelling on situations, decisions, or problems. While reflection and contemplation can be valuable for personal growth and problem-solving, overthinking can lead to becoming stuck in a loop of negative thoughts, hindering progress and preventing the identification of viable solutions. Overthinking often involves dissecting every detail of a situation or problem, which can lead to feeling overwhelmed by the sheer volume of information and potential outcomes. This over-analysis can create a state of mental paralysis, where individuals become unable to make decisions or take action due to the fear of making mistakes or encountering negative consequences. Overthinkers tend to ruminate on past events or perceived failures, continually replaying situations in their minds and focusing on the negative aspects. This constant dwelling on past experiences can prevent individuals from learning from their mistakes and moving on, perpetuating a cycle of negativity and reinforcing self-doubt. When overthinking, individuals may fall into cognitive distortions such as catastrophizing, black-and-white thinking, or mind-reading. These distorted thought patterns can exacerbate feelings of anxiety, stress, and helplessness, further complicating the decision-making process and making it even more challenging to find effective solutions. Overthinking can heighten stress and anxiety levels by continually focusing on potential negative outcomes, worst-case scenarios, or perceived threats. This constant state of worry and uncertainty can significantly impact mental health, emotional well-being, and overall quality of life, making it difficult to think clearly and rationally about potential solutions. By becoming fixated on negative thoughts and possibilities, individuals may overlook alternative approaches or potential solutions that could lead to positive outcomes or personal growth.

Perfectionism

In a similar vein to overthinking, which can impede creative thinking and problem-solving by fixating on negative thoughts and possibilities, perfectionism also poses challenges to personal growth, mental health, and interpersonal relationships. Perfectionism, the relentless pursuit of flawlessness and excessively high personal standards, can also significantly impact an individual's personal growth, mental health, and interpersonal relationships. One of the primary ways perfectionism hinders personal growth is through the fear of failure. Perfectionists often fear making mistakes, which can lead to a reluctance to take risks or try new things. This fear of failure can prevent individuals from embracing opportunities for personal growth and self-discovery, limiting their potential and overall satisfaction with life. Another issue perfectionists face is procrastination and indecisiveness, as they constantly search for the perfect solution or ideal outcome. This constant striving for perfection can delay progress and prevent individuals from achieving their goals and aspirations. The constant pressure to achieve perfection can result in heightened stress levels, anxiety, and even burnout. The pursuit of unattainable standards can lead to chronic dissatisfaction, as perfectionists are rarely content with their achievements, always believing there is room for improvement. Furthermore, perfectionism can strain relationships, as perfectionists may extend their unrealistic expectations to others, leading to disappointment and conflict within relationships. Holding others to excessively high standards can create tension and resentment, as friends, family members, or colleagues may feel criticized or undervalued. Lastly, perfectionism can hinder creativity and innovation. The fear of failure associated with perfectionism can stifle creativity and innovation, as individuals may be less likely to experiment with new ideas or take risks. This reluctance to step outside one's comfort zone can limit personal and professional growth and hinder the ability to adapt and evolve.

Avoidance of Discomfort

Perfectionism can hold individuals back in various ways, including stifling creativity and innovation; similarly, avoidance of discomfort is another habit that can significantly impede personal growth and limit opportunities for self-improvement, as it contributes to feelings of stagnation and dissatisfaction, preventing individuals from achieving their goals and reaching their full potential. Embracing discomfort is often a prerequisite for personal growth, as challenging experiences can provide valuable learning opportunities and promote resilience. By consistently avoiding discomfort, individuals may miss out on these chances to learn, adapt, and grow. Confronting uncomfortable emotions and situations can lead to increased self-awareness and a deeper understanding of one's strengths and weaknesses. Additionally, continuously evading discomfort can reinforce fears and anxieties, as individuals may never learn to cope with challenging situations. This avoidance can contribute to increased vulnerability and decreased self-efficacy, further hindering personal growth. By consistently steering clear of discomfort, individuals may limit the range of experiences and opportunities they encounter. This restricted exposure can lead to stagnation, as individuals may struggle to broaden their horizons, develop new skills, or forge meaningful connections. Avoiding discomfort can also result in procrastination and reluctance to set ambitious goals. Individuals may choose to maintain the status quo rather than take risks or pursue challenging objectives, preventing them from achieving long-term satisfaction. In an attempt to escape discomfort, individuals may develop unhealthy coping mechanisms, such as substance abuse or excessive reliance on distractions. These maladaptive strategies can further impede personal growth and negatively impact overall health.

Recognizing and addressing these everyday negative habits is essential for promoting personal growth, and a fulfilling life. By understanding the impact of these habits on our lives and taking active steps to break free from their hold, we can pave the way for healthier, more adaptive behaviors that support our lives.

HABITS IN PERSONAL TRANSFORMATION

The science of habits is fascinating, and it all starts with the brain. When we repeat a behavior, neurons in the brain are activated and connect with one another to form new neural pathways in the brain. The more we repeat that behavior, the stronger those neural pathways become. Eventually, the behavior becomes automatic, and we don't even have to think about it. One of the most interesting things about habits is that they are triggered by cues, which are external or internal signals that tell us when to perform a behavior. For example, the sound of our alarm clock might be a cue that tells us to get out of bed, or the sight of our toothbrush might be a cue that tells us to brush our teeth. Cues can be incredibly powerful in shaping our behavior because they tell our brains when to switch into automatic mode. To effectively engage in personal transformation, it is essential to establish a mindset that supports change and growth. This mindset is characterized by openness, adaptability, and a willingness to step outside our comfort zones. By cultivating this mindset, we can better embrace the uncertainty that often accompanies change, allowing ourselves to learn from our experiences and grow as individuals. Establishing a mindset for change and growth involves several key elements:

Self-Awareness

Developing a deeper understanding of your thoughts, feelings, and behaviors is essential for personal transformation. By cultivating self-awareness, you become better equipped to recognize your patterns, identify triggers, and uncover the root causes of your habits. This heightened awareness allows you to make more conscious choices, respond to challenges more effectively, and take charge of your personal growth. Each decision you make, from your daily habits to your long-term commitments, has a cumulative effect on your overall health and life trajectory. By being mindful and purposeful in your choices, you create an environment that fosters growth and supports your transformational journey. Additionally, being conscious of your choices enables you to better align your actions with your goals and values. When you are aware of the potential consequences of each decision, you can make choices that are congruent with your desired outcomes, facilitating a more seamless and effective personal transformation. Furthermore, becoming more conscious in your choices promotes a sense of agency and empowerment as you actively shape the course of your life rather than passively allowing circumstances to dictate your path. This proactive approach can help you overcome feelings of helplessness and victimhood, enabling you to approach challenges with resilience, confidence, and optimism.

Clear Goals and Intention Setting

Personal transformation requires a clear vision of your desired outcomes and the ability to set actionable, realistic goals. This involves breaking down your long-term objectives into smaller, manageable steps and regularly monitoring your progress. Establishing clear intentions creates a roadmap for change, providing direction, motivation, and a sense of purpose as you work towards your goals. Breaking your goals into smaller steps offers numerous positive effects. First, it makes the process less overwhelming, as focusing on smaller tasks reduces the likelihood of feeling discouraged by the magnitude of your ultimate objective. Second, accomplishing these smaller tasks generates a sense of achievement, boosting your self-confidence and reinforcing your belief in your ability to reach your larger goals. Moreover, dividing your goals into incremental steps allows you to monitor your progress more effectively, enabling you to adjust your approach and strategies as needed. This flexibility helps you remain adaptable and resilient in the face of challenges, increasing the likelihood of successful personal transformation.

Support and Accountability

Change is more achievable when you surround yourself with a supportive network of individuals who share similar values and aspirations. This can include friends, family, mentors, or even online communities. Establishing a system of accountability through regular check-ins, sharing your goals with others, or working with a coach can help you stay committed and motivated throughout your personal transformation journey. When others are aware of your goals and check in on your progress, it creates a sense of responsibility and encourages you to remain consistent in your efforts. This external support reinforces your commitment and provides valuable feedback, advice, and encouragement when faced with challenges. Additionally, knowing that others are invested in your success can bolster your determination and foster a sense of camaraderie, making personal transformation more enjoyable and fulfilling.

Embracing Discomfort

Personal growth often requires stepping outside your comfort zone and confronting challenges or uncertainties. By embracing discomfort, you develop resilience, adaptability, and the ability to thrive in new situations. Acknowledge that change can be uncomfortable, but view it as an opportunity for growth and learning rather than a barrier to progress. Stepping out of your comfort and familiarity allows you to rewire your brain as you create new neural pathways and strengthen existing ones through novel experiences and the acquisition of new skills. This process of neuroplasticity enables your brain to adapt and evolve, increasing your capacity for learning and personal development. Moreover, embracing discomfort and challenging yourself helps you better understand your strengths, weaknesses, and limitations. This self-awareness is crucial in refining your purpose in life, as you can better align your actions with your values, passions, and goals. Overcoming obstacles and pushing through discomfort can also lead to a heightened sense of self-efficacy and confidence, allowing you to approach future challenges with greater resolve and determination. As you repeatedly step out of your comfort zone and expose yourself to new situations, you become more adept at navigating change and uncertainty. This skill is invaluable in today's rapidly evolving world, where adaptability and resilience are increasingly important for personal and professional success.

Persistence and Patience

Personal transformation is a gradual process that requires consistent effort and dedication. It's essential to understand that change doesn't happen overnight, and setbacks are a natural part of the journey. By cultivating patience, persistence, discipline, and dedication, you can remain committed to your goals even when faced with obstacles or challenges. Embrace the idea that progress, no matter how small, is still progress, and continue to move forward in your journey. The journey itself is the most important aspect of transformation, as each step adds to the cumulative change and growth you experience. Each milestone you reach, every lesson you learn, and every obstacle you overcome contribute to your personal evolution. To truly respect and honor this journey, it's crucial to remain patient and dedicated, as true transformation requires time and unwavering commitment. Envisioning the end goal may be easy, but putting in the work to get there is not. It's essential to differentiate between simply dreaming of change and actively pursuing it. Those who actively engage in the transformative process by demonstrating discipline, persistence, and dedication are the ones who ultimately experience the most profound and lasting growth. This is what separates the dreamers from the doers.

Reflection and Adaptation

Throughout your personal transformation journey, it's crucial to continually reflect on your experiences, assess your progress, and adapt your approach as needed. This reflective process enables you to learn from successes and setbacks, identify areas for improvement, and make informed decisions about the next steps in your journey. Regular reflection and adaptation allow you to fine-tune your strategies, maintain momentum, and ultimately achieve lasting change and personal growth. Maintaining a broader perspective and always keeping the bigger picture in mind when working towards your goals is essential. By focusing on the overarching purpose and desired outcomes of your personal transformation journey, you can ensure that every decision you make is aligned with and contributes to achieving your ultimate objectives. This long-term perspective provides clarity, motivation, and direction as you navigate the often complex and challenging process of personal growth. Seeing the bigger picture also helps you maintain balance and prioritize your time and energy effectively. By understanding how each action and decision fits within the context of your overall transformation journey, you can make more intentional choices that consistently move you closer to your goals.

As you immerse yourself in the process of breaking habits and embracing personal transformation, you will discover the power of change and the limitless potential that resides within you. By committing to this journey, you can create a life that aligns with your values and aspirations and allows you to grow, thrive, and experience greater fulfillment.

OVERCOMING REDUNDANT THOUGHT PATTERNS

Redundant thinking, also known as repetitive or circular thinking, is a mental pattern where an individual consistently rehashes the same thoughts, worries, or concerns over and over again. These thought patterns can lead to stress, anxiety, and even depression, as they often involve dwelling on negative experiences, unresolved problems, or imagined fears. To break free from this cycle and promote personal growth, it is essential to understand the underlying mechanisms that drive redundant thinking and develop strategies to disrupt and replace these thoughts with more constructive ones. The initial and most crucial step in breaking the cycle of redundant thinking is to develop a keen awareness of your thought patterns. This involves closely monitoring the thoughts that occupy your mind during various moments of the day and discerning when you engage in repetitive or negative thinking. By examining your thoughts, you can identify underlying themes, triggers, and patterns that may contribute to unproductive thinking cycles.

Common triggers for redundant thinking may include stress, uncertainty, feelings of inadequacy, or unresolved past traumas. For example, an individual experiencing high levels of stress may find themselves constantly worrying about the same issues, even if they have no immediate solution. Similarly, someone grappling with feelings of inadequacy might ruminate on past failures, perpetuating a cycle of self-doubt and negativity. To identify your triggers, engaging in self-reflection and introspection is helpful. This process may involve asking yourself questions about the circumstances or emotions that tend to precede repetitive thoughts or seeking patterns in your thought processes. Redundant thinking frequently originates from irrational beliefs or cognitive distortions that influence how we perceive and interpret reality. These distorted beliefs can contribute to excessive worry, anxiety, and negative emotions, which only exacerbate the issue. It is vital to confront and reframe these irrational beliefs systematically to break free from the cycle of redundant thinking. Begin by examining your thoughts and identifying instances where your beliefs may not be grounded in reality but instead based on unfounded fears or assumptions. For example, you might engage in all-or-nothing thinking, seeing things in black and white without acknowledging the nuances and complexities. Alternatively, you may be prone to catastrophizing, imagining the worst-case scenario in every situation, even when the likelihood of such an outcome is low.

Once you have identified the irrational beliefs underlying your redundant thinking, develop more rational and balanced perspectives. This process might involve questioning the validity of your distorted beliefs and seeking evidence to support or refute them. For instance, if you believe that you're doomed to fail at a particular task, ask yourself what concrete evidence supports this belief and whether there are counterexamples that contradict it. As you practice challenging your irrational beliefs, you may also find it helpful to reframe your thoughts using more constructive and positive language. Instead of focusing on what could go wrong, imagine potential positive outcomes or solutions to your challenges. Over time, this practice will help you cultivate a more adaptive mindset, enabling you to break free from the cycle of redundant thinking and embrace a healthier, more balanced perspective on life.

After identifying and addressing your redundant thoughts, the next step is cultivating alternative thought patterns that encourage a healthier, more optimistic mindset. This process involves actively shifting your focus from the negatives to the positives in your life, allowing you to establish new, more adaptive ways of thinking. Begin by concentrating on positive experiences, accomplishments, or personal strengths that you may have overlooked or undervalued in the past. Make a conscious effort to remind yourself of these positives daily, as doing so can help counterbalance the negative thoughts that once dominated your mind. Additionally, consider keeping a journal to record your achievements and positive experiences, which can serve as a powerful reminder of your growth and progress when faced with challenges or setbacks.

Practicing gratitude is another effective strategy for developing alternative thought patterns. Take a few moments each day to reflect on what you are grateful for, big and small. This practice can help shift your focus from what you lack to what you already have, fostering a sense of contentment. By consistently practicing these strategies, you can gradually rewire your brain to adopt alternative thought patterns that foster a more balanced and positive outlook on life. Over time, this new way of thinking will replace the redundant thought patterns that once held you back, allowing you to embrace personal growth and transformation fully.

Excessive stress and anxiety can amplify redundant thinking, making it even more critical to incorporate efficient stress management strategies into your everyday life. By managing stress effectively, you can create a more balanced emotional state that allows you to better control and overcome repetitive thought patterns. One helpful technique for managing stress is deep breathing exercises. Deep breathing, also known as diaphragmatic breathing, is a powerful technique that can help regulate your nervous system, lower your heart rate, and promote relaxation. Deep breathing encourages the use of the diaphragm, a large muscle at the base of the lungs, instead of relying on shallow chest breathing. This technique has several physiological effects that contribute to its calming effects on the body and mind. When you engage in deep breathing, you take in more oxygen, which is essential for the proper functioning of your body's cells. As you inhale, your diaphragm contracts and moves downward, allowing your lungs to expand and fill with oxygen-rich air. When you exhale, your diaphragm relaxes, pushing air out of your lungs and expelling carbon dioxide, a waste product. This exchange of oxygen and carbon dioxide helps to maintain the optimal balance of gases in your bloodstream, supporting overall health.

Deep breathing also activates the parasympathetic nervous system, which is responsible for the body's "rest and digest" response. This activation counteracts the stress response generated by the sympathetic nervous system and helps to lower your heart rate, reduce blood pressure, and relax your muscles. As a result, you may experience a greater sense of calm and relaxation, both physically and mentally. Moreover, deep breathing can help reduce the production of stress hormones, such as cortisol, and increase the release of endorphins, which are natural mood elevators and painkillers. This shift in hormonal balance can lead to improved emotional well-being and reduced stress-related symptoms. When you are in a more relaxed state, it is easier to let go of repetitive, negative thoughts and cultivate a healthier, more balanced mindset. This technique can further enhance your ability to cope with stress and improve your overall mental health. To fully experience the benefits of deep breathing, practicing the technique regularly and incorporating it into your daily routine is essential. You can engage in deep breathing exercises for just a few minutes each day or use them as a tool to manage stress during particularly challenging moments. By making deep breathing a consistent habit, you will be better equipped to regulate your nervous system, lower your heart rate, and promote relaxation, ultimately contributing to a healthier and more resilient mind.

Progressive muscle relaxation (PMR) is another widely used stress management technique that focuses on systematically tensing and relaxing different muscle groups in the body. The practice is based on the premise that physical relaxation can lead to mental relaxation, thereby reducing stress and anxiety. PMR not only helps to alleviate tension in the muscles but also increases your awareness of the physical sensations associated with stress, enabling you to recognize and manage stress more effectively. PMR involves working through different muscle groups in a specific sequence, typically starting with the feet and gradually moving up through the body. As you focus on each muscle group, you first tense the muscles for a few seconds, then release the tension and relax the muscles for a longer period, usually about 15 to 30 seconds. This alternating pattern of tensing and relaxing helps to highlight the contrast between the sensations of tension and relaxation, providing a clearer understanding of how stress manifests physically in your body. As you become more aware of the physical sensations associated with stress, you can begin to recognize early signs of tension and take proactive steps to address it. This heightened body awareness enables you to intervene before stress levels escalate, which can significantly impact your overall well-being. Furthermore, the practice of PMR can also serve as a form of mindfulness, as it requires you to direct your attention to the present moment and focus on the sensations in your body. This mindful awareness can help to quiet your mind, interrupt cycles of redundant thinking, and foster a sense of mental clarity and calm. By incorporating PMR into your daily routine or using it as a tool during particularly stressful moments, you can effectively manage stress levels, regulate your nervous system, and promote relaxation. This tool can contribute to breaking the cycle of redundant thinking and help you develop a more balanced and positive mindset. As you become more skilled in identifying and addressing stress-related physical sensations, you'll be better equipped to maintain mental and emotional well-being in the face of life's challenges.

Physical exercise is also important to manage stress as it offers numerous physical and mental health benefits. Regular physical activity has been shown to reduce stress levels and improve mood. Exercise stimulates the release of endorphins, the brain's natural "feel-good" chemicals, which can help alleviate anxiety, depression, and negative thought patterns. When you engage in physical activity, your body experiences a variety of physiological changes that contribute to stress reduction. Exercise increases blood circulation, which helps deliver oxygen and nutrients to the brain and muscles more effectively. This process helps improve cognitive function and can enhance your ability to manage stress and regulate emotions. Additionally, exercise can help lower cortisol levels, a hormone associated with stress and anxiety. Physical activity can also be a healthy distraction from repetitive thoughts and negative emotions. When you focus on the task at hand, such as lifting weights, going for a run, or practicing yoga, you are less likely to dwell on negative thoughts or engage in redundant thinking. Engaging in physical exercise allows you to shift your focus from your thoughts to your body and the present moment. As you become more physically fit and achieve your fitness goals, you may feel a greater sense of control over your life and mental health. This positive shift in self-perception can help break the cycle of redundant thinking by promoting a more optimistic outlook on life.

Incorporating these stress management techniques into your daily routine can effectively reduce stress levels and create a more balanced emotional state. As a result, it becomes easier to break free from the cycle of redundant thinking. Managing stress is crucial to personal transformation and developing a healthier mindset. By consistently practicing these techniques and adapting them to your specific needs and preferences, you can build resilience and better manage your thought patterns, ultimately leading to a more fulfilling and emotionally balanced life.

THE BODY'S ROLE IN LETTING GO OF PAIN FROM THE PAST

Our bodies have a unique capacity to store and process emotional experiences, including pain and trauma from the past. These unresolved emotions can manifest as physical symptoms or tension in the body, impacting our quality of life. Understanding the connection between the body and our emotional history is crucial to letting go of past pain and moving towards healing and personal growth. The intricate relationship between the body and mind cannot be overstated, as our emotional experiences can directly influence our physical well-being. When we encounter traumatic or painful events, our bodies instinctively react with a stress response. This response activates the sympathetic nervous system, which is responsible for the "fight or flight" reaction, preparing us for action in the face of perceived danger. During this stress response, our bodies release stress hormones such as cortisol and adrenaline. These hormones increase heart rate, blood pressure, and blood sugar levels, providing us with the energy and resources necessary to cope with a challenging situation. While these responses are essential for survival in the short term, when experienced repeatedly or over prolonged periods, they can take a toll on our bodies.

Over time, these stress responses can become deeply ingrained in our physiology, leading to chronic tension, pain, or illness. Our muscles may become tense and tight, leading to discomfort or reduced mobility. Our immune system can become compromised, making us more susceptible to infections and diseases. Furthermore, chronic stress can disrupt our sleep patterns, digestion, and overall mental health. These physical manifestations of stress and trauma serve as a testament to the powerful body-mind connection. As our emotional experiences shape our physical state, it becomes increasingly important to recognize and address the psychological aspects of our well-being. By acknowledging and working through our emotions, we can begin to heal our minds and bodies, by reducing the chronic stress responses that contribute to ongoing tension, pain, and illness.

Our bodies possess a remarkable ability to retain memories of past traumas or emotional experiences in the form of somatic memories. These memories are embedded within the body's tissues, muscles, and nervous system and are not necessarily conscious or easily accessible through traditional memory recall. Instead, they are encoded in the body as physical sensations or patterns of tension that can persist long after the original event has passed. Somatic memories can be triggered by various external and internal stimuli, such as smells, sounds, visual cues, or even specific physical sensations. These triggers can activate the stored memory, causing an individual to re-experience the associated emotional and physical sensations, often without conscious awareness of the connection to the past event. This activation can create a feedback loop of negative emotions and physical discomfort, perpetuating the cycle of pain and making it difficult to let go of past traumas. The persistence of somatic memories in the body highlights the importance of addressing both the emotional and physical aspects of healing. Traditional talk therapy may not be sufficient to release these stored memories, as they are held within the body rather than the conscious mind. As a result, incorporating body-based therapeutic approaches, such as somatic experiencing, bodywork, or movement therapies, can be beneficial in helping individuals access and release these deeply rooted memories. Doing so can break the cycle of pain and discomfort, allowing for a complete healing process and personal transformation.

One critical step in releasing pain from the past is identifying the specific areas in your body where you hold tension or discomfort, as these can manifest unresolved emotional experiences. Gaining insight into the connection between your emotional history and your physical state requires a focused approach, and there are several methods available to facilitate this process. Body scanning is a technique often used in meditation and mindfulness practices that involves systematically bringing attention to different parts of the body, starting from the top of your head and gradually moving down to your toes. As you focus on each area, observe any sensations, tension, or discomfort that may be present while also taking note of any emotions or thoughts that arise in connection with these sensations. By cultivating a non-judgmental awareness of these sensations, you can gain valuable insights into the areas where you may be holding onto past pain and, through this mindful observation, begin to release this tension. Practicing body scanning can help you develop a deeper connection with your body and foster a greater sense of self-awareness, allowing you to address and release emotional blockages more effectively over time.

Mindfulness practices, such as meditation, yoga, or tai chi, can also help you become more attuned to your body's sensations and the interplay between your emotional and physical states. By developing a heightened sense of bodily awareness, you can more readily identify patterns of tension or discomfort that may be linked to unresolved emotional experiences. Working with a trained therapist, particularly one specializing in body-centered therapies, can be invaluable in this process. These professionals can guide you through tailored exercises and therapeutic techniques designed to help you access and release stored somatic memories, facilitating a deeper understanding of the connection between your emotional history and physical pain. By employing these methods to identify the source of your pain, you can unravel the complex relationship between emotional experiences and bodily discomfort. This awareness can be the foundation for healing, allowing you to let go of past pain and embrace a more balanced and harmonious state of being.

In addition to physical techniques, engaging in emotional processing is essential to let go of past pain entirely. This practice can involve journaling, talking with a trusted friend, or engaging in practices like mindfulness or meditation. By acknowledging and processing the emotions associated with past experiences, you can begin to heal and move forward. A key aspect of letting go of past pain and moving towards healing is addressing the emotional component of your experiences. This element requires delving into your emotions, examining their roots, and engaging in various practices to process and release them. Emotional processing allows you to confront and resolve the feelings that are intertwined with past experiences, helping you to truly let go and move forward. Journaling is a powerful tool for emotional processing because it provides a safe and private space for self-expression and self-exploration. By writing down your thoughts, feelings, and experiences, you can gain deeper insights into your emotions and their underlying causes. Here are some ideas to help you harness the power of journaling for emotional processing:

Reflect on Your Emotions

The first step in using journaling for emotional processing is to reflect on your current emotional state. Begin by writing about your emotions in the present moment, exploring the depth of your feelings and the sensations they evoke within your body. Be as specific and detailed as possible in your descriptions to create a vivid picture of your emotions. For instance, instead of simply saying, "I feel sad," you could write, "I feel a heavy sadness in my chest as if a weight is pressing down on me, making it difficult to breathe. My eyes feel teary, and my heart aches with loneliness." In addition to describing the physical sensations associated with your emotions, try to identify the emotions you're experiencing and the possible triggers. For example, "I feel sad and lonely because I miss my friends and family, who live far away, and whom I haven't been able to see in a long time. The feeling intensifies when I see their photos on social media or hear about their gatherings that I cannot attend." By reflecting on your emotions in detail, you can better understand your emotional landscape and develop greater self-awareness.

Identify the Triggers

Delve deeper into your journaling by exploring the events, situations, or stimuli that trigger your emotions. Gaining a better understanding of these triggers allows you to recognize patterns in your emotional responses and develop more effective coping strategies. For instance, "I've noticed that I consistently feel anxious whenever I'm faced with public speaking opportunities or when I have to attend large social gatherings. The thought of standing in front of a crowd or mingling with unfamiliar people makes my heart race, my palms sweat, and my mind race with worries about being judged or criticized." In your writing, dissect the aspects of these situations that evoke your emotional reactions. Are there specific elements or circumstances that exacerbate your anxiety or discomfort? By identifying these factors, you can work on addressing them by seeking support, practicing skills, or developing coping mechanisms. For example, "I've realized that my anxiety is heightened when I feel unprepared for a presentation or don't know anyone at a social event. To counteract these triggers, I can practice my speech more thoroughly or try to connect with someone before the event to have a familiar face to approach." By closely examining the triggers of your emotions through journaling, you can develop a greater sense of self-awareness and take steps to minimize their impact on your emotional well-being.

Explore the Roots of Your Emotions

Look into your personal history and reflect on past experiences that might be contributing to your current emotions. This process can help you identify unresolved issues, emotional baggage, or deeply ingrained patterns that may affect your present emotional state. For instance, "I've noticed that I feel insecure in my relationships, constantly worrying that people will leave me. When I think back, I realize that my parent's divorce during my childhood may have instilled this fear in me, as it was a time when I felt abandoned and unsupported." As you explore these emotional roots, consider the impact these past experiences have had on your beliefs, values, and expectations. Write about any patterns you notice and how these experiences have shaped your emotional responses or coping mechanisms. For example, "Because of my parent's divorce, I have developed a pattern of seeking constant reassurance from my romantic partners, fearing they will leave me just like my parents did. This has led to an overdependence on others and difficulty trusting that relationships can be stable and secure." Acknowledge the influence of your past experiences, but also consider ways to actively work on healing and overcoming these emotional wounds. This approach might involve seeking therapy, engaging in self-compassion exercises, or cultivating healthier relationships. For instance, "I recognize that my childhood experiences have shaped my insecurities, but I am committed to working on them by attending therapy sessions, practicing self-love and reassurance, and building trust with my loved ones in a healthy and balanced manner." As you continue to journal about the roots of your emotions, you'll gain a deeper understanding of how your past experiences have shaped your emotional landscape. This self-awareness can empower you to make conscious decisions to address unresolved issues and work towards a healthier, more balanced emotional state. For example, "By identifying the origins of my insecurities and working on them, I can gradually let go of the pain from my past and develop a more secure sense of self. This practice will ultimately lead to more fulfilling relationships and greater emotional well-being." Remember that exploring the roots of your emotions and healing from past pain can be challenging and may take time. Be patient with yourself and practice self-compassion as you work through this process.

Using Prompts to Dive Deeper

Journaling prompts are a valuable tool for guiding your exploration of your emotional experiences and encouraging self-reflection. By posing specific questions or topics, these prompts can help you better understand your emotions, beliefs, and thought patterns. Consider the following examples of journaling prompts:

"What beliefs or assumptions am I holding onto that may be causing my negative emotions?"

This prompt encourages you to examine the underlying beliefs or assumptions that contribute to your emotional state. For example, if you feel unworthy or inadequate, consider the beliefs driving these feelings and how you might challenge them.

"What would I say to a friend experiencing the same emotions?"

By imagining what you would say to a friend experiencing similar emotions, you can gain insight into how you might offer yourself the same support and understanding. This exercise can help you develop self-compassion and empathy for your emotional experiences.

"How can I reframe my thoughts to view this situation more positively?"

This prompt invites you to consider alternative perspectives and look for positive aspects in challenging situations. For example, instead of focusing on the negative aspects of a difficult experience, consider the lessons you've learned, the personal growth you've experienced, or any positive outcomes that have emerged.

"What can I learn from this emotional experience?"

Reflecting on the lessons you can draw from your emotional experiences can help you develop resilience and emotional intelligence. By identifying the lessons learned, you can grow from your experiences and apply this knowledge to future situations.

These prompts and others like them can facilitate deeper exploration and understanding of your emotional experiences, ultimately leading to personal growth, improved emotional well-being, and greater self-awareness. You'll cultivate a deeper understanding of your emotions, thought patterns, and responses to various situations by consistently engaging with these prompts in your journaling practice. Over time, this self-knowledge can lead to lasting personal transformation, empowering you to navigate life's challenges with greater resilience and confidence.

Practice Self-Compassion

Cultivating a self-compassionate approach in journaling is essential for promoting emotional healing and personal growth. When writing about your emotions, adopt a compassionate and non-judgmental perspective. Acknowledge your feelings without harsh self-criticism, and instead, offer yourself understanding, empathy, and kindness. Recognize that everyone experiences a wide range of emotions, and it's a natural part of the human experience. For example, "It's normal to feel sad when I miss my loved ones. I am allowed to feel this way, and seeking support from others is okay. I understand that my emotions are a reflection of my love and connection to those I care about, and I can be gentle with myself during these moments of sadness." By consistently practicing self-compassion in your journaling, you'll develop a healthier relationship with your emotions and foster a greater sense of self-acceptance and emotional resilience.

Develop Action Plans

Utilize your journal as a platform for devising practical steps and strategies to address the emotions you're experiencing. By creating a plan of action, you can foster a sense of empowerment and take control of your emotional well-being. Instead of being overwhelmed by your emotions, focus on the steps you can take to overcome or manage them more effectively. For example, "To overcome my anxiety about public speaking, I can first research and enroll in a public speaking course that provides guidance and support. Next, I can set aside time each day to practice speaking in front of a mirror or recording myself to build my confidence. Additionally, I can join a local Toastmasters club to gain experience in a supportive environment." By actively engaging in problem-solving and creating a clear roadmap for addressing your emotional challenges, you'll be better equipped to handle these emotions and cultivate a sense of resilience and self-efficacy.

Track Your Progress

Make a habit of routinely revisiting your journal entries to evaluate your emotional growth and development over time. By doing so, you can gain insights into the progress you've made, the challenges you've faced, and the strategies that have been most effective in promoting your emotional healing. Reflect on the changes you've implemented in your life, the shifts in your emotional landscape, and the improvements in your overall health. Remember to acknowledge and celebrate your successes, big and small, as these achievements are powerful motivators for continued growth. As you track your progress, consider setting specific milestones or goals to work towards in your emotional healing journey. This practice can help you stay focused, committed, and accountable to yourself. Moreover, it can provide direction and purpose in your ongoing self-improvement efforts. When you reach a milestone or achieve a goal, take the time to reflect on the journey and what you've learned along the way. Use these insights to inform your future goals and personal growth endeavors.

Change doesn't arise from passively waiting for it to happen; instead, it comes from actively initiating new behaviors to foster transformation. Many of these practices may appear insignificant or irrelevant due to preconceived biases or beliefs that certain experiences are unnecessary. However, to truly transform yourself, it is essential to shed the burdens of the past hindering your growth and adopt an open, non-judgmental perspective. By embracing new experiences and challenging your own assumptions, you can break free from old patterns and create the foundation for genuine personal transformation. By consistently practicing self-reflection and progress tracking, you will cultivate a deeper understanding of your emotional experiences, patterns, and growth trajectory. This heightened self-awareness will empower you to make informed decisions, adapt your strategies when needed, and ultimately, stay committed to your emotional healing and personal transformation journey. By incorporating these practices into your emotional processing journey, you can begin to address and release the emotions associated with past pain, fostering a sense of closure and healing. As you work through this emotional terrain, you'll be better equipped to let go of the past, embrace the present, and move forward into a brighter, more balanced future.

CHRONIC STRESS AND ITS IMPACT ON BODY AND MIND

Stress is a natural part of life. We all experience it occasionally, whether due to a work deadline, a relationship issue, or a sudden unexpected event. Our bodies are incredibly complex systems, and our stress response is no exception. The Autonomic Nervous System (ANS) is a branch of the nervous system that governs involuntary bodily functions such as digestion, heart rate, and blood pressure. Furthermore, it can be classified into two subdivisions: the sympathetic nervous system (SNS) and the parasympathetic nervous system (PNS).

The sympathetic nervous system is responsible for our body's fight-or-flight response. When we perceive a threat or danger, the SNS activates, releasing adrenaline and cortisol into our bloodstream. These hormones increase heart rate, blood pressure, and respiration, preparing our body to either fight the threat or flee from it. This response is crucial for survival in threatening situations, but it can negatively affect our health if it becomes chronic. Chronic activation of the SNS can lead to various physical and mental health problems, including hypertension, heart disease, anxiety, and depression. Studies have shown that individuals who experience chronic stress have higher levels of cortisol in their bloodstream, indicating that their SNS is chronically activated. This chronic activation of the SNS can also lead to the depletion of stress hormones, such as cortisol, and contribute to a state of chronic stress and burnout. On the other hand, the parasympathetic nervous system helps to counteract the effects of the sympathetic nervous system by promoting relaxation and rest. When activated, the PNS slows our heart rate and breathing, lowers our blood pressure, and promotes digestion and healing. The PNS is like the calm after the storm, allowing our bodies to rest and recover from the stress response.

Imagine you're sitting in a boat on a calm lake, enjoying the peaceful tranquility of the water. Suddenly, a strong gust of wind comes out of nowhere, causing your boat to rock back and forth. Your body tenses up, your heart races and your breathing becomes rapid. This reaction is your body's natural stress response, kicking into gear to help you navigate the unexpected turbulence. But what happens when that stress becomes chronic? When your body is constantly battling against the waves instead of resting in the stillness of the water? The effects can be detrimental to both your physical and mental health.

One of the ways that stress affects our brains is through the hypothalamus pituitary adrenal (HPA) axis. This axis is a series of interactions between endocrine glands in the brain and the kidney that controls the body's reaction to stress. When our brain detects a stressful situation, the HPA axis is instantly triggered and releases a hormone called cortisol, which primes the body for instant action. However, high levels of cortisol over long periods can have a negative impact on our brains. The adrenal glands produce cortisol hormone as a response to stress. In small amounts, cortisol is beneficial for the body as it helps to regulate metabolism, blood sugar levels, and blood pressure. However, when cortisol levels remain elevated over time, it can hurt our health.

Chronic stress increases the activity level and a number of neural connections in the amygdala, the brain's fear center. As cortisol levels rise, electric signals in the hippocampus, which is the part of the brain associated with learning, memories, and stress control, worsen. The hippocampus also hinders the activity of the HPA axis, so when it becomes weaker, so does our ability to control our stress. Excessive cortisol levels can also lead to a reduction in brain size, which results in the loss of synaptic connections between neurons and shrinkage of the prefrontal cortex, the part of the brain that regulates behaviors like concentration, decision-making, judgment, and social interaction.

The effects of stress may even filter right down to our brain's DNA. For instance, a study on rats revealed that the level of nurturing offered by a mother rat plays a role in determining how that baby will respond to stress later in life. The pups of nurturing moms developed a reduction in the sensitivity of stress because their brains produce more cortisol receptors, which bind to cortisol and decrease the stress response. The pups of inattentive moms had the opposite outcome and became more sensitive to stress throughout life. These changes are referred to as epigenetic, as they impact the expression of genes without directly modifying the genetic code. The changes can be reversed if the mothers are swapped. Nevertheless, a single mother rat's epigenetic changes were passed down to numerous generations of rats after her, implying that the effects were heritable.

Our understanding of stress and its impact on our bodies and brains has deepened significantly through scientific research. Stress is not just a feeling but a tangible biological event with both immediate and long-lasting impacts. The intricate web of our body's reactions to stress, from the involvement of the autonomic nervous system to the release of hormones like cortisol, reveals just how profound these effects can be. While stress is a natural part of existence, learning to master and manage it is key to preserving our overall physical and mental health. We cannot eliminate stress entirely, but with a deeper understanding of its workings, we can navigate its waves with more resilience, enabling us to enjoy the calm waters of life more fully.

EPIGENETICS
Chapter Three

HOW YOUR ENVIRONMENT TRANSFORMS YOUR GENES

Epigenetics is the study of the mechanisms that regulate gene expression without altering the underlying DNA sequence. The term "epigenetics" comes from the Greek prefix "epi-", meaning "above" or "on top of" and "genetics," referring to the study of genes. This field has gained significant attention in recent years due to the growing evidence that epigenetic changes can influence various aspects of human health, including the effects of emotional states on gene expression. To understand epigenetics, one must first understand the basic structure and function of DNA. DNA is composed of nucleotide sequences that code for genes, which are the blueprints for proteins. Gene expression, or the process of translating genes into proteins, is regulated by several mechanisms. Epigenetic modifications can be heritable, meaning they can be passed on to offspring without altering the DNA sequence. Various factors, including environment, lifestyle, and emotional states, can influence these modifications.

Epigenetic mechanisms are like tiny switches that can turn our genes on or off without changing the DNA. Think of a light switch in a room – the wiring (DNA) stays the same, but you can control whether the light is on or off. The two main epigenetic mechanisms are DNA methylation and histone modification. Imagine your DNA as a lengthy sentence made of words (genes). Methylation is like putting a piece of tape over a word, making it unreadable. When a gene is "taped over" (methylated), it can't be used to create proteins, which are the building blocks of our body. Removing the tape (demethylation) allows the gene to be active again. Your environment and emotions can influence which genes get "taped over." Now picture your DNA as a lengthy thread coiled around tiny cylindrical structures called histones. These histones assist in maintaining the organization of the DNA. By altering the shape of the histones (through a process known as histone modification), the accessibility of genes to be read and utilized can be increased or decreased. Similar to methylation, both your environment and emotions can play a role in determining how these histones are modified.

Your emotions can affect which genes are turned on or off through these epigenetic mechanisms. When stressed, your body can change the "tapes" and "cylinders" in your DNA. This process might cause stress-response genes to be more active, making you feel even more stressed. Over time, these changes can lead to anxiety, depression, or other stress-related issues. If someone goes through tough times as a child, such as being mistreated or ignored, their "tapes" and "spools" can be changed to make them more vulnerable to mental health problems later in life. This shows that our experiences, even in early life, can have a lasting impact on our DNA. On the other hand, when you're happy or relaxed, your body can change the "tapes" and "spools" in a positive way. This could help your immune system work better and reduce inflammation, making you healthier overall. The connection between emotional states and gene expression through epigenetic mechanisms highlights the importance of mental health. Interventions aimed at improving emotional states, such as stress reduction techniques, psychotherapy, and mindfulness practices, can potentially lead to beneficial epigenetic changes, promoting better health outcomes.

EXPLORE THE BODY'S RESPONDS TO POSITIVE AND NEGATIVE EMOTIONS

Epigenetics provides a valuable framework for understanding the complex relationship between emotions and physical health. This field allows us to examine how emotions can influence epigenetic processes and gain insights into their long-term effects on well-being. Positive emotions such as happiness, love, and gratitude can contribute to improved physical health through various epigenetic mechanisms. For example, individuals who experience positive emotions tend to have longer telomeres, the protective caps at the ends of chromosomes that shorten with age and stress. This discovery is likely due to epigenetic changes that affect the expression of genes responsible for maintaining telomere length, promoting cellular health and longevity. They have a crucial function in preserving the consistency and stability of our genetic data throughout the process of cell division. As cells divide over time, telomeres gradually become shorter, eventually resulting in cellular senescence and an increased susceptibility to age-related illnesses. Telomerase is an enzyme that plays a role in preserving telomere length by appending repeated DNA sequences to chromosome ends, thereby offsetting the innate process of telomere shortening. Research has demonstrated that practicing mindfulness meditation can lead to increased telomerase activity. By cultivating a non-judgmental awareness of the present moment and promoting positive emotions, mindfulness meditation can help reduce stress and its harmful effects on our bodies at the cellular level. Stress contributes to the shortening of telomeres and a decrease in telomerase activity. Therefore, by mitigating the stress response through mindfulness practice, we can preserve telomere length and promote healthier aging. Increased telomerase activity resulting from mindfulness meditation may also be linked to the positive psychological effects of the practice. It is suggested that these positive psychological states might help promote healthier gene expression, which in turn can lead to increased telomerase activity and improved cellular health.

Positive emotions can also reduce inflammation by altering the expression of genes associated with inflammatory processes. This occurs through epigenetic changes, such as decreased DNA methylation and altered histone modifications, which can lead to the suppression of pro-inflammatory genes. For example, experiencing feelings of love and social connection has been shown to decrease the expression of pro-inflammatory genes, potentially lowering the risk of chronic inflammation-related conditions like heart disease. On the other hand, negative emotions, including stress, anxiety, and anger, can have detrimental effects on physical health by influencing epigenetic processes. Chronic stress can lead to lasting epigenetic changes, particularly in genes related to the stress response, such as the glucocorticoid receptor gene. These changes can result in an excessive or prolonged stress response, increasing the risk of stress-related disorders. A study on children exposed to early-life stress, such as abuse or neglect, showed lasting epigenetic changes in their glucocorticoid receptor gene. These changes were associated with an increased risk of developing mental health disorders like depression and anxiety later in life.

Anxiety can also influence epigenetic processes that regulate the expression of genes involved in neurotransmitter systems, such as serotonin and dopamine. Altered gene expression can contribute to imbalances in these systems, exacerbating anxiety symptoms and potentially leading to other mental health issues. Research has shown that individuals with anxiety disorders exhibit epigenetic changes in genes related to serotonin signaling, which may contribute to developing and maintaining anxiety symptoms. By examining how emotions influence epigenetic processes, we gain a better understanding of their long-term effects on physical well-being.

MASTERING GENE EXPRESSION THROUGH PERCEPTION AND CONSCIOUSNESS

We often believe that our genes and environment determine our characteristics and health. However, recent scientific advances have revealed that our perception plays a significant role in gene expression. This knowledge empowers us to understand that we are not mere victims of our genes or environment but rather masters of controlling gene characteristics. Our bodies are intricate systems that constantly interact with a diverse range of signals from various sources. These signals can profoundly impact our physical and mental health, influencing cellular processes and overall health. Understanding the different types of signals and their effects can provide valuable insights into maintaining and improving our well-being.

Pharmaceutical drugs, for example, are specifically designed to interact with certain proteins, enzymes, or receptors within the body in order to induce desired changes. These drugs can either enhance or inhibit the activity of target molecules, thus influencing cellular functions and leading to therapeutic effects. The use of medications for treating various conditions, such as reducing inflammation, managing pain, or regulating blood pressure, demonstrates the power of targeted drug therapy in promoting health and alleviating disease symptoms. In addition to pharmaceutical drugs, our bodies also respond to energy signals in our environment. Electromagnetic fields (EMFs), which include radio waves, microwaves, and visible light, can interact with our cells and tissues, affecting their function. While low-level exposure to EMFs is generally considered safe, excessive exposure to certain types of EMFs, such as ionizing radiation from X-rays, may harm our health, potentially leading to DNA damage and increased cancer risk.

Light, another form of energy signal, plays a crucial role in regulating various physiological processes within our bodies. For instance, exposure to sunlight helps stimulate the production of vitamin D, essential for maintaining healthy bones and immune function. Furthermore, exposure to natural light regulates the body's internal circadian rhythms, ensuring proper sleep-wake cycles and influencing hormone release, digestion, and other vital processes. Importantly, our thoughts and emotions can also serve as signals that influence our well-being.

Energy signals around and within us constantly influence matter, including our bodies. You can think of the human body as an orchestra, where cells and tissues are the musicians, and energy fields act as the conductor, guiding the harmony and balance of the overall performance. These energy fields, like the electrical signals in our nervous system and the electromagnetic fields produced by our heart, help coordinate and regulate the functions of our cells, impacting our overall health.

At the quantum level, particles display properties of both waves and particles, similar to how water can take the form of both liquid and solid ice. This concept, known as wave-particle duality, suggests that matter and energy are two sides of the same coin, with one able to transform into the other. Consequently, our thoughts and beliefs about matter and energy can influence how our cells and DNA interact with external signals, just like adjusting the volume or tone of a musical instrument can change the quality of the sound it produces. By understanding the connection between DNA, proteins, and the materialization of features in our bodies, we gain a deeper appreciation of the power of our perception in shaping our lives. Our consciousness, thoughts, and emotions can directly influence gene expression, ultimately affecting our health. By recognizing the vital role our perception plays in controlling gene characteristics, we can take charge of our health, foster positive emotions and beliefs, and harness the potential of our minds to shape our reality.

GENERATIONAL KARMA AND THE TRANSFER OF EMOTIONS

Emotions play a crucial role in shaping human behavior. They influence our thoughts, actions, and physiological responses and can potentially affect future generations' emotions and health. In recent years, research has shed light on how emotions can be passed down through generations and how they can impact our genes. Parents' emotional experiences, both good and bad, can shape their children's emotional development. For example, if a parent is often stressed or anxious, it might cause changes in their genes that are passed on to their children. On the other hand, a loving and nurturing environment can lead to positive changes in genes that help children become more emotionally resilient. These changes can be caused by environmental factors, including emotions, and may even be passed down through generations. So, if a mom experiences a lot of stress during pregnancy, her child might have a higher chance of being stressed too, because of changes in how their stress-related genes work.

Animal studies have shown that emotions can also be passed down through generations. For example, researchers found that when they trained mice to be afraid of a specific smell, the mice's children and even their grandchildren were also afraid of the same smell. This fear was passed down through changes in the mice's genes, which shows that emotional experiences can directly impact genetic information. People who have lived through traumatic events, like wars or natural disasters, may also pass down the effects of that trauma to their children and grandchildren. This is called the intergenerational transmission of trauma. Studies have found that the children of people who experienced significant trauma may have a higher risk of emotional difficulties and mental health issues. The reason could be because the trauma led to changes in the parent's genes, which were then passed down to the next generations. Moreover, it's important to note that the intergenerational transmission of trauma doesn't just have negative consequences. It also serves as a way for organisms to adapt to their environment by passing on crucial information about potential threats, thereby improving the chances of survival for future generations. Overall, the intergenerational transmission of trauma highlights the complex relationship between our genes, emotions, and environment, shedding light on the intricate ways in which our experiences can shape our lives and those who come after us.

One fascinating aspect of epigenetics is its potential connection to the concept of generational karma. Generational karma refers to the notion that the consequences of an individual's actions, thoughts, and emotions can ripple through generations, affecting the lives of their descendants. The idea of generational karma stems from ancient wisdom traditions that believed in the interconnectedness of all living beings. According to these traditions, the actions and emotions of an individual can have lasting effects on the lives of their descendants. Modern epigenetic research has provided scientific evidence for this age-old belief, showing that our ancestors' experiences can leave an imprint on our genes. These epigenetic changes can then be passed down through generations, influencing our physical health, emotional well-being, and even our predispositions to certain behaviors.

The intergenerational transmission of trauma is a prime example of how generational karma may manifest in our lives. Epigenetic changes caused by traumatic experiences can be inherited by subsequent generations, increasing their risk of emotional difficulties and mental health issues. However, generational karma is not limited to negative experiences; positive behaviors, such as regular exercise and healthy eating habits, can also lead to beneficial epigenetic changes that can be passed down to future generations. Breaking the cycle of generational karma involves understanding the root causes of these inherited patterns and consciously choosing to make positive changes in our lives.

The first step in breaking generational karma is cultivating self-awareness. Becoming aware of the patterns passed down to you involves exploring your family history, discussing recurring issues with family members, and engaging in self-reflection to identify behaviors or emotions that may have originated from your ancestors. By understanding these patterns, you can address them effectively and make positive changes in your life. Emotional healing is essential when confronting generational karma. Identifying the patterns stemming from your family history is only the beginning; addressing the underlying emotional wounds is crucial. This healing process may involve seeking professional help, such as therapy or counseling, participating in support groups, engaging in mindfulness meditation or journaling to process and release unresolved emotions.

Making conscious lifestyle changes can help create beneficial epigenetic changes. Adopting a healthy diet, engaging in regular exercise, practicing stress-reduction techniques, and fostering positive relationships can all break the cycle of inherited patterns. Shifting your mindset and beliefs about generational karma is also crucial. Recognize that you have the power to break free from inherited patterns and create a new path for yourself and future generations. Cultivating a growth mindset that embraces change and self-improvement can be a transformative experience.

Engaging in spiritual practices such as meditation, yoga, or prayer can help you connect with your inner wisdom and find guidance in breaking the cycle of generational karma. These practices can also foster a sense of interconnectedness and compassion for yourself and others, allowing you to release negative patterns more easily. By integrating these practices into your daily life, you can create lasting change and positively impact your life and the lives of those around you.

Lastly, if you are a parent or plan to become one, being aware of the potential impact of generational karma on your children can help you make conscious choices in your parenting style. During pregnancy, the developing fetus is highly sensitive to environmental factors that can shape its epigenome – the collection of chemical changes to the DNA and histone proteins that regulate gene expression. These factors include the mother's diet, stress levels, exposure to toxins, and overall health. A mother's diet during pregnancy has significant epigenetic implications for the developing fetus. The availability of vital nutrients, such as folate, vitamin B12, and choline, can influence DNA methylation patterns in the child's genes. Adequate intake of these nutrients is crucial for proper fetal development and can help reduce the risk of birth defects, such as neural tube defects. On the other hand, a poor maternal diet lacking these essential nutrients can lead to abnormal methylation patterns and potentially increase the risk of developmental disorders or long-term health issues in the child.

Prenatal Stress during pregnancy can also have lasting epigenetic effects on the developing child. High levels of maternal stress have been linked to altered DNA methylation patterns in the child's genes, which can result in an increased risk of cognitive, emotional, and behavioral issues later in life. Prenatal stress has also been associated with a higher risk of preterm labor and low birth weight. Managing stress during pregnancy through relaxation techniques, regular exercise, and social support can help minimize the potential epigenetic consequences for the child.

Exposure to environmental toxins, such as air pollution, tobacco smoke, and certain chemicals, can also have epigenetic effects on the developing fetus. These toxins can alter the child's epigenome, leading to changes in gene expression that may increase the risk of various health issues, including asthma, obesity, and neurodevelopmental disorders. Reducing exposure to environmental toxins during pregnancy is essential for the child's long-term health.

The epigenetic changes that arise during pregnancy can persist throughout the child's life and even into subsequent generations. However, epigenetic modifications are also influenced by the child's environment and experiences during early life, including nutrition, stress, and social interactions. Early interventions, such as promoting a balanced diet, providing a nurturing and stimulating environment, and minimizing exposure to toxic substances, can help support healthy epigenetic patterns and promote optimal child development.

Encourage open communication, emotional expression, and resilience in your children to help them break free from inherited patterns. This intentional parenting approach can significantly affect your children's and future generations' well-being. The way parents raise and interact with their children can play a role in how emotions are passed down through generations. If a child has a strong, loving bond with their parent, they are more likely to grow up emotionally healthy. But if a child has a problematic relationship with their parent, they may be more likely to struggle with emotional problems later in life. These different parenting styles can lead to changes in children's genes. Emotions have a powerful impact on our health and the well-being of our children and grandchildren. By understanding the ways emotions can be passed down through generations and affect our genes, we can work towards creating a more supportive and nurturing environment for future generations, promoting emotional resilience and overall health.

ENVIRONMENTAL FACTORS IN THE PROGRESSION OF HUMAN RACES

It is essential to explore epigenetics' role in the human race's development and how their environments have shaped their unique characteristics and behaviors. One vital aspect to consider is that the environment plays an influential role in shaping the genetic expression of a population. Over time, different populations have adapted to their surroundings in response to various stressors, including climate, food availability, and local pathogens. These adaptations have led to the development of unique genetic traits that promote survival in specific environments. These traits are passed down through generations, creating a unique set of characteristics that define each race.

For example, populations living in regions with high exposure to sunlight have developed darker skin pigmentation, an evolutionary adaptation that provides protection against the harmful effects of ultraviolet (UV) radiation. Conversely, populations in areas with limited sunlight exposure have lighter skin tones to optimize the production of vitamin D, which is essential for bone health and immune system function. In addition to physical adaptations, epigenetics have also shaped the cultural evolution of different races. Cultural practices, including dietary habits, social norms, and traditional medicine practices, can influence gene expression. These factors can create epigenetic changes that can be passed down through generations, thereby shaping the identity of different racial and ethnic groups.

Diet is a significant factor that can influence gene expression. The types of food consumed by different populations vary according to regional availability and cultural preferences. For instance, people of East Asian descent often consume rice and soy-based foods, while those of Mediterranean descent have diets rich in olive oil, fish, and fresh vegetables. These dietary differences can lead to epigenetic changes that affect the expression of genes related to metabolism, immune response, and overall health. For example, the traditional Mediterranean diet is rich in omega-3 fatty acids and antioxidants, which have been shown to positively affect the expression of genes associated with inflammation and cardiovascular health. As a result, populations following this diet may have a lower risk of developing heart disease and other chronic conditions.

Social norms, such as family structure and social support, can also influence gene expression by affecting an individual's stress levels and mental health. For example, strong social bonds and community ties have been shown to protect against stress and its negative health consequences. In some cultures, the importance of extended family networks and intergenerational living arrangements can create a supportive environment that reduces stress, thereby influencing the expression of genes related to stress response and mental health.

Traditional medicine practices have been passed down through generations and are deeply ingrained in the cultural fabric of many racial and ethnic groups. These practices can also impact gene expression, particularly when it comes to stress response and immune function. For instance, traditional Chinese medicine emphasizes the importance of maintaining balance and harmony within the body, often using herbal remedies and acupuncture. These practices can influence gene expression by modulating the immune system and reducing inflammation, which can, in turn, affect overall health.

The racial makeup of one's DNA is the result of generations of ancestral experiences and adaptations to specific environments. This genetic diversity has shaped the physical appearance and cultural practices, beliefs, and values of different populations. For example, the Inuit people, who have lived for thousands of years in the Arctic, have unique genetic adaptations that enable them to efficiently metabolize fats for energy. This genetic trait is linked to their traditional diet, which is rich in fatty fish and marine mammals.

The unique challenges faced by different populations have led to the emergence of distinct behaviors, thought processes, and emotional patterns, which have been passed down through generations via epigenetic mechanisms. The intersection of genetics and cultural practices has shaped the identity of different racial and ethnic groups. By understanding the unique genetic and cultural heritage that shapes their identity, individuals can gain a deeper appreciation for their ancestry and the factors that have contributed to who they are today. Moreover, recognizing the complex interplay between genetics, culture, and environment can foster greater empathy and understanding between different racial and cultural groups, promoting a more inclusive and harmonious society.

For example, populations that have experienced a history of hardship and scarcity, such as the Armenian people, may develop a cultural emphasis on resourcefulness, adaptability, and resilience. Armenians have faced numerous challenges throughout their history, including the Armenian Genocide in 1915, political instability, natural disasters, wars, and economic hardships. As a result, the Armenian people have developed a strong sense of unity and a culture that values perseverance, adaptability, and community support. These traits can be reinforced through epigenetic mechanisms, perpetuating these characteristics within the population. For instance, research has shown that exposure to traumatic events can result in epigenetic changes that affect stress response and coping mechanisms. Consequently, the Armenian people, having experienced collective trauma, may have inherited epigenetic markers contributing to their resilience and ability to overcome adversity. Furthermore, the Armenian diaspora, which has dispersed Armenians all over the world, has contributed to the development of a global Armenian community. This sense of belonging and cultural pride has helped Armenians maintain their unique identity, despite geographical distance and assimilation into various societies. The strong ties to their heritage, combined with their adaptive nature, have allowed them to preserve their traditions and values while also integrating into their new environments.

Conversely, populations that have enjoyed relative abundance and stability may develop different cultural values and behaviors. These groups may place greater emphasis on individualism, material wealth, and self-expression, as opposed to the collective well-being and survival-focused mindset observed in populations with a history of hardship. However, it is important to note that these characteristics are not mutually exclusive. Many populations exhibit a combination of traits shaped by a diverse range of historical, cultural, and environmental influences.

Epigenetics research uncovers an intriguing connection between environmental factors and the evolution of human populations. The unique challenges and opportunities faced by different populations have shaped their actions, thoughts, and emotions in culturally and biologically significant ways. Understanding the complex interplay between epigenetics and the environment can provide valuable insights into the rich diversity of human experience and help foster greater empathy and understanding between different racial and cultural groups.

NEUROPLASTICITY
Chapter Four

THE WONDERS OF NEUROPLASTICITY

The groundbreaking concept of neuroplasticity has revolutionized our understanding of the human brain, revealing its remarkable ability to adapt and change in response to experiences, thoughts, and emotions. Neuroplasticity refers to the brain's capacity to reorganize and adapt its structure, function, and connections, allowing for ongoing growth and change throughout an individual's life. Several fundamental mechanisms drive this adaptive capacity, including synaptic plasticity, neurogenesis, and cortical remapping.

Synaptic plasticity refers to the strengthening or weakening of synaptic connections between neurons, which can enhance or diminish the efficiency of neural communication, ultimately affecting learning and memory processes. Neurogenesis, on the other hand, involves the generation of new neurons, particularly in specific brain regions such as the hippocampus, which plays a crucial role in learning and memory functions. This continuous generation of neurons allows the brain to maintain its cognitive abilities and adapt to new information and experiences. Lastly, cortical remapping is the process by which the brain's cortical regions reorganize themselves, allowing different areas to take over the functions of damaged or underutilized regions. This ability to reassign functions to alternative brain regions is essential for recovery and rehabilitation from brain injuries and neurological disorders. Synaptic plasticity, neurogenesis, and cortical remapping enable the human brain to remain flexible and adaptive, facilitating learning, memory, and overall cognitive function throughout an individual's life.

One of the primary drivers of neuroplasticity is experience. As individuals engage in various activities and encounter new experiences, their brains undergo changes in response to these stimuli. This experience-dependent plasticity enables the brain to adapt and optimize its functioning to better meet the demands of the individual's environment and experiences. For example, musicians who practice a specific instrument for hours daily often show increased neural connections and cortical thickness in brain regions associated with auditory processing and fine motor control. When the musician starts learning the instrument, the brain establishes new connections among neurons, facilitating the transmission of information related to playing the instrument. These connections strengthen over time, allowing the musician to develop a high level of expertise and proficiency. As the musician continues practicing, the brain undergoes structural changes, such as the growth of dendritic spines and the formation of new synapses, contributing to the overall increase in neural connectivity. This increase in connectivity is a direct result of the brain adapting to the demands of the musician's environment and experiences, enabling them to play their instrument with greater precision and skill.

In addition, repetitive practice also leads to changes in the brain's functional organization. For example, as the musician becomes more proficient at playing their instrument, the brain allocates more resources to the specific regions associated with the relevant skills, such as auditory processing and fine motor control. Consequently, these brain areas become more efficient at processing information related to the musician's instrument, further enhancing their performance. Overall, the process of neuroplasticity in the musician's brain illustrates the remarkable ability of the human brain to adapt and evolve in response to environmental stimuli and individual experiences, ultimately refining the skills and abilities of the individual.

Emotional experiences can also shape the brain through neuroplasticity, with positive emotions promoting the formation of new neural connections and enhanced cognitive abilities, while chronic stress and negative emotions can impair neuroplasticity and contribute to cognitive decline. Furthermore, neuroplasticity plays a crucial role in recovery and rehabilitation from brain injuries and neurological disorders, as the brain's capacity to rewire and adapt following an injury can facilitate the restoration of lost functions and skills. As the brain adapts and reorganizes itself in response to injury, it can form new connections and pathways to compensate for damaged areas, restoring lost functions and skills. Stroke patients who undergo rehabilitation often experience improvements in motor function and cognitive abilities due to the brain's capacity to rewire and adapt following the injury.

One primary mechanism of neuroplasticity is synaptic plasticity, which involves changes in the strength and efficiency of synaptic connections between neurons. Synaptic plasticity is crucial for learning and memory, as it allows the brain to encode new information and experiences by modifying the communication patterns between neurons. Two fundamental forms of synaptic plasticity are long-term potentiation (LTP) and long-term depression (LTD). LTP is the process of strengthening synaptic connections, leading to increased efficiency in neural communication, whereas LTD is the weakening of synaptic connections, reducing the efficiency of neural communication. LTP and LTD are essential in refining neural circuits and optimizing brain function. Another important mechanism of neuroplasticity is structural plasticity, which involves changes in the physical structure of neurons and their connections. Structural plasticity can manifest in various forms, including the growth of new neurons (neurogenesis), the formation of new dendritic spines (the branches on neurons that receive synaptic input), and the extension or retraction of axons (the long projections of neurons that transmit electrical signals). These structural changes contribute to the brain's capacity for adaptation and resilience, enabling it to reorganize and repair itself in response to injury, disease, or environmental changes. Experience-dependent plasticity is another crucial aspect of neuroplasticity, emphasizing the role of environmental stimuli and experiences in shaping the brain's organization and function. This form of plasticity can be observed in both synaptic and structural changes, as the brain responds to new experiences by modifying neural connections and reorganizing neural circuits. Experience-dependent plasticity is particularly evident during early development when the brain is highly sensitive to environmental stimuli and undergoes rapid changes in response to the experiences it encounters. The mechanisms of neuroplasticity are also influenced by various factors, including age, genetics, and environmental factors. For example, age-related changes in the brain's structure and function can impact neuroplasticity, with younger individuals typically displaying a greater capacity for neural adaptation and growth. Genetic factors can also influence neuroplasticity, as certain genetic variations may predispose individuals to enhanced or reduced plasticity. Additionally, environmental factors such as stress, nutrition, and exposure to toxins can impact neuroplasticity, either promoting or hindering the brain's capacity for change and growth.

Understanding the concept of neuroplasticity empowers individuals to harness its potential for personal growth and development. Individuals can enhance their cognitive abilities, emotional well-being, and overall brain health by engaging in activities that promote neuroplasticity, such as learning new skills, practicing mindfulness, and maintaining an active lifestyle.

Neuroplasticity is a remarkable feature of the human brain

that allows it to adapt and change in response to our experiences, thoughts, and emotions. By understanding and harnessing the power of neuroplasticity, we can take charge of our brain health and actively shape our cognitive and emotional well-being.

NURTURING THE ADAPTIVE BRAIN ACROSS THE LIFESPAN

Neuroplasticity, or the brain's ability to change and adapt, is a continuous process that occurs throughout our lives. During early development, the brain experiences rapid and extensive changes, with new neural connections forming at an incredible pace. This period, known as the critical period, is marked by heightened neuroplasticity, which allows the brain to be particularly sensitive and responsive to environmental stimuli. Simultaneously, the brain undergoes a process of synaptic refinement, wherein unused connections are pruned away to optimize neural networks for efficiency and adaptability. The brain's heightened sensitivity to environmental influences means that experiences can profoundly impact an individual's cognitive, emotional, and social development. Positive experiences, such as exposure to rich learning environments, secure attachment to caregivers, and engagement in social interactions, can foster healthy brain development and promote resilience, cognitive abilities, and emotional well-being.

On the other hand, adverse experiences, such as neglect, abuse, or exposure to chronic stress, can disrupt the development of crucial neural networks and have long-lasting consequences on mental health, cognitive functioning, and overall well-being.

As we transition into adulthood, neuroplasticity remains an essential aspect of our brain's capacity for learning, memory, and adaptation. Contrary to earlier beliefs that adult brains were relatively fixed and unchanging, research has demonstrated that the adult brain retains the ability to form new neural connections and reorganize existing ones in response to new experiences and challenges. This ongoing neuroplasticity enables us to acquire new skills, adapt to novel situations, and cope with life's various changes. Adult neuroplasticity plays a particularly important role in the context of skill acquisition and expertise development. When we learn a new skill or hone an existing one, our brains undergo structural and functional changes that support the demands of specific tasks and activities. This may involve strengthening synaptic connections between neurons or even creating new ones, allowing the brain to optimize its performance in response to the skill's unique requirements. Adult neuroplasticity is essential for coping with the challenges and changes that life inevitably brings.

As we age, encounter novel situations, or experience injuries or illnesses, our brains can adapt and reorganize to maintain optimal functioning. This capacity for adaptation becomes particularly important in rehabilitation following brain injury or neurological disorders, as it allows the brain to compensate for damaged areas and restore lost functions to some extent.

Over time, the brain experiences various structural and functional changes that can impact neuroplasticity. These changes may include a reduction in overall brain volume, decreased synaptic density, and altered neurotransmitter systems. Despite these natural age-related changes, it is crucial to understand that a decline in neuroplasticity is not an unavoidable fate. Numerous studies have demonstrated that engaging in mentally stimulating activities, maintaining social connections, and adopting a healthy lifestyle can help preserve and even enhance neuroplasticity in older adults. Mentally stimulating activities, such as learning new skills, solving puzzles, reading, or engaging in creative pursuits like painting or writing, can promote the formation of new neural connections and help maintain cognitive function. These activities challenge the brain and encourage it to adapt and grow, counteracting the natural decline that may occur with aging. Maintaining social connections is another key factor in preserving neuroplasticity. Social interactions provide the brain with a rich array of stimuli that support cognitive function and emotional well-being. Engaging in regular social activities, such as joining clubs, volunteering, or spending time with friends and family, can help keep the brain active and foster a sense of belonging and purpose, all of which contribute to a healthier brain. Adopting a healthy lifestyle is also essential for promoting neuroplasticity in older adults. This includes regular physical exercise, which has been shown to increase blood flow to the brain, support the growth of new neurons, and improve cognitive function. A well-balanced diet, rich in fruits, vegetables, whole grains, lean proteins, and healthy fats, can provide the essential nutrients for optimal brain health.

Cognitive reserve is a significant concept related to aging and neuroplasticity, referring to the brain's ability to adapt and compensate for age-related changes by utilizing existing cognitive resources more efficiently or recruiting alternative neural pathways. This concept suggests that the brain has a certain level of resilience, allowing it to maintain cognitive function despite challenges such as aging, brain injury, or neurodegenerative diseases. Several factors contribute to an individual's cognitive reserve, including education, occupation, and engaging in intellectually stimulating life activities. Higher levels of education have been linked to increased cognitive reserve, as the learning process helps to build and strengthen neural connections. Likewise, intellectually demanding occupations can contribute to cognitive reserve by providing ongoing cognitive challenges that stimulate the brain, promoting the formation and maintenance of neural connections.

Cognitive reserve can help protect against age-related cognitive decline and even delay the onset of neurodegenerative diseases like Alzheimer's. Research has shown that individuals with higher cognitive reserve tend to experience less cognitive decline as they age and may be less likely to develop Alzheimer's disease or other forms of dementia. This protection arises because the brain can draw upon its cognitive reserve to compensate for age-related changes or damage, allowing it to maintain cognitive function despite these challenges.

Neuroplasticity is a dynamic process that occurs throughout the entire lifespan, from the rapid changes during early development to the more subtle adaptations that take place in adulthood and aging. Understanding the factors that influence neuroplasticity across the lifespan can help us devise strategies to promote cognitive health, improve learning and memory, and maintain our capacity for adaptation and resilience in life's challenges.

REWIRING THE BRAIN FOR POSITIVE CHANGE

Negative patterns and habits can be deeply ingrained in our brains, affecting our thoughts, emotions, and behavior. However, by leveraging the power of neuroplasticity, we can create new neural connections to override these old negative patterns and foster positive change in our lives. Negative patterns can manifest as repetitive negative thoughts, unhealthy emotional responses, or destructive behaviors. These patterns are often deeply ingrained in the brain, reinforced by years of repetition and conditioning. Understanding their neural basis is essential to override these negative patterns. The brain's plasticity means that negative patterns are not fixed, and it is possible to create new neural connections that can help to break free from them.

The first step to creating new neural connections is identifying the areas where negative patterns have taken hold in your life. This self-reflection can help you determine which thought patterns, emotional responses, or behaviors you wish to change, providing a starting point for your journey toward rewiring your brain. Mindfulness can play a crucial role in creating new neural connections. By becoming more aware of our thoughts, emotions, and sensations, we can learn to identify negative patterns as they arise and choose to engage in healthier responses. Regular mindfulness practice, such as meditation, can strengthen the neural pathways associated with self-awareness, emotional regulation, and attention, ultimately promoting positive patterns. Mindfulness is the key that brings your mind and body in complete harmony by realigning every aspect of your being.

The human brain has an incredible capacity for growth and change; engaging in new experiences and learning new skills is one way to tap into this potential. When we take on new challenges, we expose ourselves to unfamiliar stimuli that can stimulate the brain to form new neural connections. By engaging in new experiences, we can also break free from old, negative patterns that may be holding us back. This is because the brain is highly adaptable and can reorganize itself in response to new information and experiences. For example, individuals with anxiety disorders may develop negative thought patterns and avoidance behaviors that perpetuate their anxiety. However, by exposing themselves to new situations and confronting their fears, they can gradually create new neural pathways that help them overcome their anxiety.

It's important to note that creating new neural connections requires effort and persistence. The brain is a complex and constantly evolving system, and forming new pathways can be challenging. However, by consciously engaging in new experiences and learning new skills, we can stimulate neuroplasticity and promote the growth of new neural connections that can help us override old negative patterns. Furthermore, as we continue to challenge ourselves and engage in new experiences throughout our lives, we can promote ongoing growth and development of the brain, leading to improved cognitive function.

Another approach is to actively challenge negative thought patterns by replacing them with positive ones. When we experience positive emotions, our brains release neurotransmitters such as dopamine and serotonin, which can strengthen neural connections and promote the formation of new ones. These positive emotions can also help to reduce stress and negative emotions, which can have detrimental effects on the brain's neural connections. Practicing gratitude, for example, has been shown to increase activity in the prefrontal cortex, a region of the brain associated with positive emotions and decision-making. Similarly, engaging in acts of kindness or volunteering can activate the brain's reward centers and promote the release of neurotransmitters that enhance positive emotions. Building strong social connections can also have a profound effect on our brain's neural connections. Studies have shown that individuals with strong social support systems have greater emotional resilience and cognitive functioning and a reduced risk of developing cognitive decline later in life. By actively seeking out experiences that evoke positive emotions and fostering social connections, we can create new neural pathways that prioritize positive thoughts and feelings, helping to override old negative patterns.

Consistency is key, and the more we engage in healthy behaviors, the more natural they become, ultimately leading to the creation of new, positive habits that can replace old, negative ones. With time and dedication, these new pathways can become the brain's default mode, effectively overriding the old patterns that no longer serve us and promoting a healthier, more fulfilling life.

THE PLACEBO EFFECT
Chapter Five

THE PLACEBO EFFECT AND THE POWER OF THE MIND

The human mind has long been considered one of the most powerful tools at our disposal. Our thoughts, beliefs, and perceptions shape our reality in profound ways, influencing not only our mental health but also our physical health. The placebo effect is a testament to the incredible influence our thoughts and beliefs can have on our physical and emotional well-being.

A placebo is an inactive substance or treatment used as a control to compare the effects of an experimental intervention. The placebo effect refers to the phenomenon in which people experience an improvement in their symptoms or condition, not due to the inherent properties of the placebo but rather because of their beliefs and expectations about the treatment. The power of the placebo effect has been demonstrated in a wide range of conditions, from pain management to depression, anxiety, and even Parkinson's disease. The effect can be so potent that, in some cases, the improvement observed in patients receiving the placebo is comparable to those receiving the actual medication. The placebo effect is a clear demonstration of the power of belief in shaping our experiences and outcomes. When individuals believe that a treatment will be effective, their faith in it can lead to measurable changes in their symptoms and overall health. This effect is not limited to the realm of medicine; our beliefs can influence our performance in various aspects of life, such as academics, sports, and personal relationships.

The concept of the placebo has been a subject of fascination and controversy throughout history. From its earliest appearance in ancient civilizations to its current status in modern medicine, our understanding of the placebo effect has evolved significantly. The origins of the placebo effect can be traced back to ancient civilizations, where healers and medicine men relied on the power of suggestion, ritual, and faith to treat various ailments. Using substances with no inherent healing properties, such as colored water, was common in these early medical practices. The belief in the efficacy of these treatments often resulted in improvements in patients' conditions, a phenomenon we now recognize as the placebo effect.

The term "placebo" was first used in a medical context in the late 18th century. English physician William Cullen coined the term to describe treatments intended to please rather than cure the patient. Over time, placebos in medicine evolved from soothing patients to a method for controlling the psychological effects of treatment in clinical trials. In the early 20th century, as the scientific method gained prominence in medicine, researchers began to understand the importance of controlling for variables in experiments. Placebos became a critical tool in this process, serving as a neutral comparison group for evaluating the true effects of a treatment. In 1946, the first double-blind, placebo-controlled clinical trial was conducted by British anesthesiologist Sir Henry K. Beecher. This groundbreaking study compared the effects of the analgesic drug morphine and a placebo in treating postoperative pain. The double-blind design, in which neither the patients nor the researchers knew who was receiving the active treatment, helped to eliminate bias and establish the true efficacy of the drug. Beecher's work laid the foundation for the widespread use of placebo-controlled trials in modern medical research. Today, these trials are considered the gold standard for evaluating the safety and effectiveness of new treatments and interventions.

As placebo-controlled trials became more common, researchers began to uncover the complex psychological mechanisms underlying the placebo effect. Early research focused on the role of patients' expectations in shaping their experiences of treatment. It was found that when patients believed they were receiving an effective treatment, they often reported improvements in their symptoms, even when the treatment was a placebo. Further research has explored the factors contributing to the placebo effect, such as conditioning, the doctor-patient relationship, and the power of suggestion. The growing body of evidence has led to a deeper understanding of the placebo effect as a complex interplay of psychological, social, and neurobiological factors.

THE PLACEBO EFFECT IN THE BRAIN AND THE BODY

The placebo effect is more than just a figment of our imagination; it has a tangible impact on the brain. Expectation plays a crucial role in the placebo effect. When individuals anticipate a positive outcome from treatment, their brains release specific neurotransmitters and activate neural pathways that can lead to actual physiological changes. These changes can result in the alleviation of symptoms, even without an active treatment.

Several brain regions have been implicated in the placebo effect. Key areas include the prefrontal cortex, the anterior cingulate cortex, the insula, and the amygdala. These regions are involved in various aspects of the placebo effect, such as processing expectations, emotional regulation, and the perception of pain. The prefrontal cortex plays a significant role in forming and processing expectations. It helps to integrate information from various sources, such as past experiences and contextual cues, to create predictions about the outcomes of a treatment. The anterior cingulate cortex is involved in the regulation of pain and emotional responses. This region is activated when individuals experience pain relief due to a placebo treatment, suggesting a direct role in mediating the placebo effect on pain perception. The insula is responsible for processing interoceptive information, which is information related to the body's internal state. It has been implicated in modulating the placebo effect on pain and other bodily sensations. The amygdala is involved in processing emotional responses and has been shown to play a role in the placebo effect, particularly in anxiety and fear.

Several neurotransmitters mediate the placebo effect, including dopamine, endorphins, and serotonin. These neurotransmitters are involved in various aspects of the placebo effect, such as pain relief, mood regulation, and reward processing. Dopamine is a key neurotransmitter in the brain's reward system. It has been shown that dopamine release is increased in response to a placebo treatment, particularly when the individual expects a rewarding outcome. This increase in dopamine levels can contribute to the positive effects of the placebo treatment. Endorphins are natural pain-relieving compounds produced by the brain. They are released in response to various stimuli, such as stress, exercise, and placebo treatments. The release of endorphins can reduce pain perception and an overall sense of well-being, contributing to the placebo effect. Serotonin is a neurotransmitter involved in mood regulation and has been implicated in the placebo effect on depression and anxiety. The expectation of a positive outcome from a treatment can increase serotonin levels, resulting in improved mood and reduced anxiety.

The placebo effect has been shown to induce neuroplastic changes in the brain, which can contribute to the long-term effects of the treatment. These changes can occur at various levels, such as alterations in the strength of neural connections, the formation of new connections, and changes in the expression of genes related to neural function. The placebo effect influences the brain and also has far-reaching implications for the rest of the body. The immune system plays a crucial role in defending the body against pathogens and maintaining overall health. Research has shown that the placebo effect can influence the immune system in various ways, such as modulating the release of cytokines and altering the activity of immune cells. These changes can directly impact an individual's health. One study found that participants who believed they were receiving an immune-boosting medication showed an increase in the activity of natural killer cells, a type of immune cell that plays a crucial role in fighting infections and cancer. This finding suggests that the expectation of improved immunity can lead to actual changes in immune function.

Hormones are chemical messengers that regulate various physiological processes, such as growth, metabolism, and stress responses. The placebo effect can influence hormonal regulation by altering the release of hormones like cortisol, adrenaline, and oxytocin. Cortisol is a stress hormone that regulates blood sugar, inflammation, and immune function. Studies have shown that the placebo effect can reduce cortisol levels, contributing to reduced stress and improved immune function. Adrenaline, also known as epinephrine, is a hormone involved in the fight-or-flight response. The placebo effect can modulate the release of adrenaline, influencing heart rate, blood pressure, and other physiological processes. Oxytocin is a hormone that plays a role in social bonding, trust, and relaxation. The placebo effect has been shown to increase oxytocin levels, which can contribute to improved mood.

One of the most well-studied aspects of the placebo effect is its impact on the perception of pain. Placebo treatments have significantly reduced pain in various conditions, such as postoperative pain, migraines, and chronic pain disorders. Research has also demonstrated that the placebo effect on pain is influenced by various factors, such as the individual's expectations, the context in which the treatment is administered, and the nature of the placebo itself. For example, a study found that participants who received a placebo treatment in the form of an expensive-looking cream reported more significant pain relief than those who received the same treatment in a less visually appealing package.

While the placebo effect refers to the positive outcomes associated with sham treatment, the nocebo effect is the opposite phenomenon: negative outcomes arising from negative expectations or beliefs. The nocebo effect can worsen symptoms and manifest adverse effects, even when no active treatment is administered. Like the placebo effect, the nocebo effect can influence various physiological processes, such as immune function, hormonal regulation, and pain perception. This phenomenon highlights the importance of addressing patients' expectations and beliefs in clinical settings to minimize the potential for negative outcomes.

The placebo effect is a powerful demonstration of the influence of our thoughts and beliefs on our brain and body. By understanding the neural mechanisms underlying this phenomenon, we can better appreciate the potential applications of the placebo effect in medicine and personal development.

SUGGESTIBILITY AND ITS IMPACT ON PLACEBO RESPONSES

Suggestibility refers to the degree to which an individual is susceptible to accepting and incorporating the suggestions, ideas, or beliefs of others. It can be defined as the propensity of an individual to accept and internalize suggestions, beliefs, or ideas from external sources, such as authority figures, peers, or the media. It is a complex psychological trait that can be influenced by various factors, including an individual's personality, cognitive style, and social context.

Several factors can influence an individual's level of suggestibility. Personality traits, such as openness to experience, have been linked to increased suggestibility, while individuals with high levels of skepticism or critical thinking may be less susceptible to suggestions. Cognitive factors, such as attention, working memory, and executive functioning, can also impact an individual's suggestibility, with people with stronger cognitive abilities potentially being more resistant to external suggestions. The social environment can play a significant role in shaping an individual's suggestibility. Individuals may be more likely to accept suggestions from authority figures or people they perceive as experts. Similarly, social norms and peer pressure can also influence suggestibility. An individual's emotional state can impact their level of suggestibility, with heightened stress or anxiety potentially making a person more susceptible to suggestions.

Suggestibility plays a critical role in the placebo effect, as individuals more susceptible to suggestions may be more likely to experience positive outcomes from placebo treatments. Research has shown that suggestibility can influence the magnitude of the placebo effect, with highly suggestible individuals experiencing more significant symptom improvement than those with lower suggestibility. Understanding one's suggestibility can be beneficial for personal growth and development. By recognizing the factors influencing our susceptibility to suggestions, we can make more conscious decisions about the information and ideas we accept and incorporate into our beliefs and behaviors.

Furthermore, suggestibility can be harnessed for self-improvement through autosuggestion, which involves intentionally giving oneself positive suggestions or affirmations to promote desired changes in thoughts, emotions, or behaviors. Suggestibility is a complex psychological trait that can significantly impact an individual's thoughts, beliefs, and behaviors. It plays a crucial role in phenomena such as the placebo effect and can be harnessed for personal growth and development. By understanding and embracing our suggestibility, we can make more informed decisions about the ideas and beliefs we adopt and use this trait to enhance and personal growth.

OVERCOMING OBSTACLES AND EMBRACING CHANGE

One of the primary obstacles to harnessing the power of the placebo effect is the presence of limiting beliefs, which can prevent us from fully embracing the potential of our minds to influence our reality and health. Limiting beliefs are deeply ingrained thoughts or assumptions that constrain our potential and hinder our ability to achieve our goals. These beliefs can be rooted in our upbringing, past experiences, or societal conditioning. They often operate subconsciously, influencing our thoughts, emotions, and behaviors without conscious awareness.

Self-doubt is a pervasive and often debilitating limiting belief that can significantly impact an individual's ability to reach their full potential. It involves questioning one's capabilities, intelligence, or worthiness and can manifest in various aspects of life, including personal, professional, and health-related pursuits. Self-doubt can be particularly damaging when it comes to harnessing the power of the placebo effect, as our beliefs and expectations play a crucial role in determining the efficacy of a treatment or intervention.

Several factors can contribute to the development of self-doubt in an individual. Childhood experiences can significantly shape an individual's self-perception and beliefs about their abilities. For instance, a child constantly criticized or compared unfavorably to others may develop a deep-seated sense of inadequacy, manifesting as self-doubt later in life. Experiencing failures or setbacks can lead to self-doubt, particularly when these negative experiences are internalized and taken as evidence of one's incompetence. This can create a cycle of self-doubt, where an individual fears future failures and consequently avoids taking risks or pursuing new opportunities. Comparing oneself to others, particularly those who are perceived as more successful or capable, can fuel self-doubt. This comparison trap can lead to feelings of inadequacy, as individuals may believe they are lacking in some way compared to their peers.

Perfectionism is a double-edged sword, as it can drive individuals to achieve high standards but also contribute to self-doubt. When perfectionists set unrealistic expectations for themselves, they may experience a heightened sense of self-doubt when they inevitably fall short of these expectations. Imposter syndrome is a psychological phenomenon where individuals question their accomplishments and fear being exposed as a fraud. This persistent self-doubt can prevent individuals from recognizing their true capabilities and embracing the power of the placebo effect.

To combat self-doubt and unlock the potential of the placebo effect, individuals must first acknowledge and confront their limiting beliefs. Additionally, surrounding oneself with supportive and encouraging people can help counteract self-doubt and foster a more positive self-image. By cultivating self-confidence and belief in one's abilities, individuals can tap into the power of the placebo effect and experience its many benefits in promoting healing.

Some individuals may be skeptical about the idea that their thoughts and beliefs can have a tangible impact on their physical health. This type of skepticism stems from a lack of understanding or disbelief in the connection between mental and emotional states and their impact on physical health. People skeptical of the mind-body connection may doubt the effectiveness of mental and emotional interventions in promoting healing, which can ultimately undermine the power of the placebo effect in their lives.

Several factors can contribute to skepticism about the mind-body connection in an individual. A predominant factor is the influence of Western medical culture, which has historically focused on the biomedical model of health and disease. This model emphasizes the role of physical factors, such as genetics, pathogens, and biochemical imbalances, in determining health outcomes. As a result, individuals raised in this culture may be more inclined to view physical and mental health as separate entities, leading to skepticism about the role of the mind in affecting physical well-being. Another factor contributing to skepticism about the mind-body connection is a lack of exposure to or understanding of scientific research supporting this concept. Numerous studies have demonstrated the powerful influence of the mind on physical health, such as the effects of stress on the immune system or the role of emotions in pain perception. However, individuals unfamiliar with this research may be more likely to dismiss the mind-body connection as pseudoscience or wishful thinking.

Personal experiences or anecdotes can also shape an individual's beliefs about the mind-body connection. For example, someone who has tried alternative healing modalities without experiencing any perceived benefits may become skeptical of the mind-body connection and the potential for mental and emotional interventions to affect their physical health. Similarly, witnessing others fail to achieve healing through mind-body practices may reinforce this skepticism. In some cases, skepticism about the mind-body connection can be rooted in fear of taking personal responsibility for one's health. Accepting the mind-body connection implies that one's thoughts, emotions, and beliefs can influence their physical well-being, which can be intimidating for some individuals. This fear can lead to resistance or skepticism, as it may be more comfortable to attribute health outcomes solely to external factors, such as medical treatments or genetic predispositions. To overcome skepticism about the mind-body connection and harness the power of the placebo effect, individuals can educate themselves about the wealth of scientific research supporting this concept. Engaging with this research can help shift perspectives and foster an understanding of the strong interconnection between mental and physical health.

The fear of failure or disappointment can lead to a reluctance to embrace the power of the placebo effect. This fear can manifest as an excessive concern about the potential negative outcomes of a situation, such as failing to achieve a desired goal or disappointing oneself or others. When fear of failure is present, it can create a self-fulfilling prophecy, where the fear itself contributes to the undesired outcome, diminishing the potential benefits of treatments or interventions. Past experiences of failure, particularly in situations where the stakes were high, or the consequences were significant, can lead to the development of fear of failure. For example, an individual who has tried various treatments for a chronic condition without success may fear trying new approaches, as past failures have caused disappointment and frustration.

High expectations from parents, peers, or society can also contribute to developing a fear of failure. An individual raised in an environment where success is highly valued, and failure is seen as a sign of weakness may be more likely to develop this fear, as the pressure to succeed can be overwhelming. An individual with low self-esteem may be more likely to develop a fear of failure, as they may doubt their abilities and worth. This lack of self-confidence can lead to a heightened fear of failing, as the individual may believe they are incapable of achieving success. Habitual negative self-talk, where an individual consistently tells themselves they are incapable or deserving of success, can reinforce the fear of failure. This self-defeating mindset can create a cycle of self-doubt, further perpetuating the fear and limiting the power of the placebo effect.

To conquer the fear of failure and tap into the potential of the placebo effect, individuals can develop a growth mindset, which involves viewing challenges as opportunities for growth and learning rather than threats to their self-worth. Embracing the concept that failure is a natural part of the learning process can help to reduce the fear associated with it. Engaging in self-reflection and identifying the root causes of one's fear of failure can be essential in overcoming this self-limiting belief. By understanding the sources of this fear, individuals can address the underlying issues and develop strategies to manage their fear more effectively, ultimately enhancing their ability to harness the power of the placebo effect.

To overcome these limiting beliefs and harness the power of the placebo effect, it is fundamental to cultivate self-awareness, challenge negative thought patterns, and develop a growth mindset. By identifying and addressing these obstacles, individuals can tap into the mind's remarkable potential to influence their reality and promote healing.

BRAINWAVES
Chapter Six

UNDERSTANDING BRAINWAVES AND THEIR SIGNIFICANCE

Brainwaves are electrical patterns produced by the neurons in your brain. These patterns vary in frequency and amplitude and are measured in Hertz (Hz). The different types of brainwaves (Figure 4) are associated with different states of consciousness, ranging from deep sleep to heightened awareness. The five main types of brainwaves are alpha, beta, gamma, theta, and delta. Alpha waves have a frequency of 8-12 Hz and are typically associated with relaxed and calm mental states. They are often present when you are in a meditative or reflective state. Beta waves, on the other hand, have a frequency of 12-30 Hz and are associated with alertness, focus, and concentration. They are often present when you are engaged in a task that requires cognitive effort, such as studying or problem-solving. Gamma waves have a frequency of 30-100 Hz and are associated with heightened states of consciousness and peak performance. They are often present during moments of insight, creativity, and inspiration. Theta waves have a frequency of 4-8 Hz and are associated with a deep state of relaxation and meditation. They are also present during the early stages of sleep and can be associated with dream states. Delta waves have the lowest frequency, typically below 4 Hz, and are associated with deep, restorative sleep. They are present when the body is most relaxed and can be related to the release of growth hormones and other restorative processes.

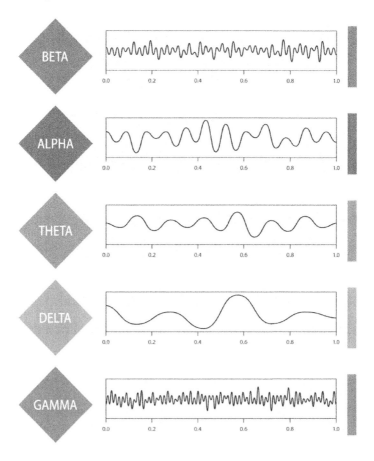

Figure 4: The Human Brainwaves.

Understanding the different types of brainwaves can help you better understand your own mental and emotional states. By recognizing which type of brainwave you are currently in, you can take steps to consciously shift your state of consciousness. For example, if you are feeling stressed or anxious, try meditating to shift from a high-beta state to a more relaxed alpha or theta state. Or, if you are feeling creatively stuck, you should engage in activities that can stimulate gamma waves, such as brainstorming or engaging in artistic expression. Transitioning from the alpha brainwave state to the delta brainwave state is an essential part of the sleep-wake cycle. When you wake up in the morning, your eyes detect light. This information is sent to a small region in your brain called the suprachiasmatic nucleus (SCN), located in the hypothalamus. The SCN regulates the body's circadian rhythm or internal clock. It signals the pineal gland to stop producing melatonin and start producing serotonin, which is associated with the alpha brainwave state. The alpha brainwave state is a relaxed but alert state of mind associated with creativity, visualization, and problem-solving. This state is often induced during meditation, hypnosis, or daydreaming. When you are in the alpha brainwave state, your brain is more receptive, making it easier to learn new things and absorb information.

As the day progresses and your brain perceives less light, the SCN signals to the pineal gland to start producing melatonin, which is associated with the delta brainwave state. The delta brainwave state is the slowest and is associated with deep sleep and restorative processes. When you are in the delta brainwave state, your brain is almost completely shut down, and the body can focus on repairing tissues, strengthening the immune system, and consolidating memories. Maintaining a healthy sleep-wake cycle is essential, as disruptions to this cycle can lead to various health problems such as insomnia, depression, and anxiety. Maintaining a healthy sleep-wake cycle is recommended for maintaining a healthy sleep schedule, avoid stimulants such as caffeine and alcohol before bedtime, and create a relaxing sleep environment.

During meditation, you can consciously shift your brainwaves to the alpha or theta state by relaxing your body, slowing your breathing, closing your eyes, and blocking out external stimuli. When you enter the alpha state, your brainwave frequency slows to a range of 8 to 13 Hz. This state is characterized by a relaxed but alert state of mind. You are aware of your surroundings but are more focused on your inner world than your outer world. This state allows you to tap into your subconscious mind, access your creativity, and find solutions to problems. Meditation in the theta state is often experienced when you are drifting off to sleep or in a deep state of relaxation, like during hypnosis. Theta brainwaves have a frequency range of 4 to 7 Hz. This state is characterized by a deep sense of calm and peace, where the mind is completely free of distractions and thoughts. In the theta state, you are more likely to experience vivid mental imagery, intuition, and access to your subconscious mind. This state is beneficial for creative visualization, accessing more profound levels of self-awareness, and connecting with your inner self. Shifting your brainwaves consciously to the alpha or theta state during meditation has numerous benefits. It can help reduce stress, increase focus and creativity, improve sleep quality, boost your immune system, and promote overall mental and physical health.

Gamma brainwaves are high-frequency brainwaves with a frequency range of 30 to 100 Hz, making them the fastest of all the brainwave states. They are often called the "superconscious" state because of their remarkable effects on the human mind and body. Gamma brainwaves are believed to be associated with synchronizing different parts of the brain, allowing for a more unified and holistic approach to processing information. When gamma brainwaves are present, the brain can process information more quickly and efficiently. People often report feeling an increased sense of awareness and heightened perception of the world around them. In this state, individuals may also experience a feeling of "oneness" with the universe or a sense of spiritual connection. This feeling of connection can lead to powerful positive emotions, such as love, joy, and gratitude, which are associated with gamma brainwaves. Studies have shown that people who experience higher levels of gamma brainwaves are often more creative, empathetic and have greater cognitive flexibility. These individuals also tend to have more positive moods, greater compassion for others, and better mental health. Research has linked increased gamma brainwave activity to improved memory, enhanced focus and attention, increased compassion and altruism, and a reduction in stress and anxiety.

Several ways to increase gamma brainwave activity include deep meditation, yoga, and other mindfulness practices. Regular practice of these techniques has been shown to increase gamma brainwave activity, leading to greater feelings of connectedness, improved cognitive function, and enhanced emotional well-being. Certain brain training exercises and biofeedback devices can also increase gamma brainwave activity in the brain, providing a powerful tool for personal growth and transformation.

SYNCHRONIZATION OF THE BRAIN

Synchronization of brain activity is crucial for optimal brain function and overall health. The good news is that the brain can be trained to synchronize through various techniques, including meditation, mindfulness practices, biofeedback, neurofeedback, and other brainwave training methods.

Meditation is one of the most effective ways to synchronize the brain. When you meditate, you focus your attention on a specific object, thought, or breath, which helps to calm the mind and slow down brain activity. As you continue to practice meditation, your brain becomes more adept at entering into a state of coherence, in which different regions of the brain begin to work together in a synchronized manner. Research has shown that regular meditation can lead to structural changes in the brain, including increased gray matter in areas associated with attention, memory, and emotion regulation. These changes have been linked to improved cognitive function and emotional regulation.

Biofeedback is a technique used to help individuals gain

greater control over their physiological processes by providing them with real-time information about their bodily functions. During biofeedback sessions, electrodes or sensors are attached to various body parts to monitor physiological responses such as heart rate, breathing, and muscle tension. The information collected by the sensors is then fed back to the individual in real time, either through visual or auditory signals. Through this process, individuals can learn to recognize the physical cues associated with different mental and emotional states, such as stress or anxiety, and develop strategies to control their responses. For example, a person suffering from chronic pain may learn to reduce muscle tension and breathing rate to lessen the intensity of the pain. Alternatively, someone with high blood pressure may learn to regulate their breathing and heart rate to help reduce their blood pressure. Biofeedback treats various conditions, including anxiety, depression, migraines, chronic pain, and hypertension. In a study, biofeedback was found to be effective in reducing symptoms of depression and anxiety in patients with major depressive disorder. Another study found that biofeedback effectively reduced the frequency and severity of migraines.

Neurofeedback, on the other hand, is a technique that involves measuring brainwave activity and providing feedback to the user in real time. During neurofeedback, electrodes are placed on the scalp to measure the brain's electrical activity, and the data is displayed on a computer screen. The electrodes detect the electrical signals produced by the neurons in the brain, which are recorded and amplified by the electroencephalogram (EEG) machine. The signals are then displayed on a computer screen or recorded on a chart in the form of a graph, which shows the amplitude and frequency of the brainwaves. The goal is to improve coherence in the brain and optimize brain function. During neurofeedback, individuals are trained to produce specific patterns of brainwave activity by rewarding the brain for producing desired patterns of activity and providing feedback when the brain produces undesired patterns of activity. This feedback can come in the form of visual or auditory cues, such as a sound or a game, which respond to changes in brainwave activity.

During an EEG recording, the subject sits in a comfortable chair or lies on a bed. Then the electrodes are attached to the scalp using a conductive gel or paste. The electrodes are placed in specific locations on the scalp according to the 10-20 system, a standard system used to ensure consistent electrode placement across subjects. Once the electrodes are in place, the subject is asked to remain still and relaxed with their eyes closed for several minutes while their brain activity is recorded. The EEG machine records the electrical signals produced by the neurons in the brain and displays them on the computer screen or chart. The user can then see their brainwave patterns and receive feedback on how to alter their brainwaves to achieve a desired state. Individuals can improve their cognitive function and emotional regulation by learning to control their brainwaves.

Neurofeedback can help individuals with various conditions, such as ADHD, anxiety, depression, and chronic pain. It can also be used to improve cognitive function and enhance athletic performance. In addition, neurofeedback has been found to increase the synchrony between different brain regions, leading to improved communication and coordination between brain networks. Both biofeedback and neurofeedback are effective techniques for synchronizing the brain and improving cognitive function and emotional regulation.

THE POWER OF LUCID DREAMING

Lucid dreaming, the phenomenon of becoming aware that one is dreaming while still in the dream state, has long fascinated both researchers and the general public. This unique state of consciousness allows individuals to exert some degree of control over their dreams, enabling them to explore their inner world, confront fears, and practice skills. The significance of lucid dreaming lies in its potential to positively impact personal growth, creativity, and skill development, particularly for professionals and athletes who seek to hone their abilities in a controlled environment.

One of the most intriguing aspects of lucid dreaming is the brain's inability to distinguish between real and imagined experiences. When individuals engage in a task or activity, whether in waking life or within a lucid dream, the brain activates similar neural networks, allowing for comparable learning and skill development in both contexts. This brain characteristic has garnered considerable attention from professionals and athletes, who have recognized the potential benefits of lucid dreaming for their respective fields. For athletes, the controlled environment of a lucid dream offers a unique opportunity to practice their skills without the constraints of physical limitations or the risk of injury. Within a lucid dream, athletes can rehearse specific movements, visualize successful outcomes, and experiment with novel techniques while enjoying the advantages of a risk-free, immersive environment. This mental rehearsal can complement physical training, reinforcing neural pathways associated with the desired skill and enhancing overall performance. Numerous athletes across various disciplines, such as gymnastics, skiing, and basketball, have reported using lucid dreaming to refine their skills, overcome performance-related anxieties, and gain a competitive edge.

Professionals in other fields can also benefit from the unique opportunities afforded by lucid dreaming. For instance, musicians can use lucid dreaming to practice their instruments, experiment with new compositions, or overcome stage fright. Similarly, public speakers can rehearse presentations and develop strategies to manage anxiety, while artists can explore their creativity and generate new ideas within the limitless landscape of their dreams. Despite its potential benefits, lucid dreaming remains an elusive skill for many individuals. However, various techniques have been developed to help increase the likelihood of experiencing lucid dreams. By incorporating these practices into their daily routines, individuals can cultivate the necessary skills and mindset for lucidity in the dream state.

One such technique is reality testing, which involves

regularly checking whether one is dreaming or awake throughout the day. This can be accomplished by performing simple tasks, such as trying to push a finger through the palm of the hand or questioning the logical consistency of one's environment. By repeatedly engaging in these reality checks, individuals train their minds to question the nature of their surroundings, increasing the likelihood of recognizing the dream state when it occurs. Dream journaling is another effective technique for enhancing lucid dreaming. By consistently recording the content of their dreams upon waking, individuals can improve their dream recall and identify recurring patterns or themes. This heightened awareness of one's dreams can facilitate the recognition of the dream state and foster the ability to become lucid. Additionally, reviewing the dream journal can help individuals set specific intentions for their next lucid dream experience, such as practicing a skill or confronting a fear.

Mnemonic induction of lucid dreams (MILD) is a technique that involves setting an intention before falling asleep to remember that one is dreaming. This can be done by repeating a mantra, such as "I will realize I am dreaming," while visualizing oneself becoming lucid within a dream. The MILD technique works by utilizing prospective memory, which is the ability to remember to perform an action in the future. The use of external devices has also been explored as a means to facilitate lucid dreaming. Some devices, such as specialized masks or headbands, are designed to detect rapid eye movement (REM) sleep, the stage of sleep most closely associated with dreaming. Once REM sleep is detected, these devices emit subtle visual or auditory cues, such as flashing lights or gentle sounds, intended to alert the dreamer that they are in a dream without fully waking them. These cues can help individuals recognize the dream state and achieve lucidity with practice.

The significance of lucid dreaming extends beyond mere novelty or curiosity, as it offers a unique and powerful tool for skill development, personal growth, and creativity. By harnessing the power of lucid dreaming, professionals and athletes can tap into a vast reservoir of untapped potential, honing their skills and overcoming barriers in a controlled, immersive environment. As the mysteries of lucid dreaming continue to unravel, the possibilities for enhancing performance, fostering creativity, and promoting psychological well-being may become increasingly apparent, transforming how we approach learning, growth, and self-discovery.

MEDITATION
Chapter Seven

THE TIMELESS PRACTICE OF MEDITATION

Throughout history, individuals have sought methods to attain inner peace, enhance self-awareness, and develop a deeper comprehension of themselves and their surroundings. Meditation has been an essential instrument in this quest for millennia, originating in ancient spiritual and religious customs. Meditation has gained traction in recent decades as people seek strategies to cope with the demands of contemporary life, alleviate stress, and enhance their mental and emotional well-being. Meditation is a potent practice that can transform lives by fostering mindfulness, presence, and self-awareness. It is an ability that can be honed through regular practice and commitment. As interest in meditation increases, so does scientific research to understand its effects on the brain, body, and overall well-being. Delving into the current state of scientific knowledge on meditation will offer a solid foundation for integrating meditation into one's daily routine. By comprehending the scientific rationale for meditation and the variety of practices available, you will be better prepared to incorporate meditation into your life and experience its transformative power. With patience, dedication, and a readiness to explore the depths of the human mind, anyone can embark on this life-changing journey.

Meditation's origins can be traced back to ancient cultures worldwide, including India, China, and Egypt, among others. These early meditation practices were frequently inextricably linked to religious and spiritual beliefs, reflecting the desire to connect with the divine or achieve a deeper understanding of the self and the world. The earliest documented evidence of meditation dates back to around 1500 BCE, found in the ancient Indian scriptures known as the Vedas. These scriptures, which form the foundation of Hinduism, contain hymns, rituals, and philosophical teachings that address various aspects of meditation. Meditation practice in India evolved as different spiritual and philosophical systems, such as Buddhism and Jainism, emerged with their unique meditation techniques. Around the 6th and 5th centuries BCE, Siddhartha Gautama, later known as the Buddha, introduced a form of meditation called "mindfulness" or "insight" meditation, focusing on observing the present moment with non-judgmental awareness. This practice formed the foundation of Buddhist meditation, which eventually spread across Asia and the rest of the world.

At the same time, meditation practices were being developed within Taoism in China. This philosophical and religious tradition emphasizes harmony with the natural world and the cultivation of inner peace. Taoist meditation practices like Qigong and Tai Chi combine breath control, visualization, and movement to achieve equilibrium and harmony between mind, body, and spirit. In ancient Egypt, texts from around 2000 BCE describe practices similar to meditation, involving calming the mind, concentrating on the breath, and chanting sacred words or phrases. These practices facilitated communication with the divine and assisted in spiritual transformation. Meditation also played a role in the spiritual practices of other ancient civilizations, such as the Greek mystery schools and the indigenous cultures of the Americas. These early forms of meditation often involved rituals, chanting, and altered states of consciousness to connect to higher realms or achieve a deeper understanding of the self and the cosmos.

In the Western world, meditation practices began to gain popularity in the 20th century, particularly with the rise of the New Age movement and the growing interest in Eastern spirituality. In recent decades, scientific research has uncovered numerous physical and mental health benefits associated with meditation, further fueling its popularity in the West. Various forms of meditation, have been adapted for secular use and integrated into modern healthcare and educational settings.

The history and origins of meditation reveal a rich tapestry of spiritual and philosophical traditions from around the world. As meditation continues to evolve and adapt to the needs of modern society, it remains a powerful practice for cultivating inner peace.

THE POWER OF BEING IN THE PRESENT MOMENT

The modern world is filled with distractions, deadlines, and demands that can overwhelm us with information and noise. In the midst of all this, it's easy to fall into a routine of going through the motions of daily life without really being present in the moment. The concept of being present, or staying in the now, is often discussed in self-help circles, but what does it really mean? Being present isn't just about physically showing up; it's about being mentally and emotionally present as well. Your body may go through the motions of your daily routine on autopilot, but your mind should be fully engaged in the present moment. That's easier said than done, especially when our minds often wander to the future or the past. So how can we master the art of being present? Many individuals turn to meditation as a tool to become more present in their daily lives. From a scientific perspective, meditation offers a new way to understand what it means to be fully present.

Multiple research efforts have explored the impact of

consistent meditation practice on the brain, revealing that it can foster a heightened sense of mindfulness and presence. One study discovered that individuals who had been meditating for approximately nine years displayed increased gray matter density in various brain regions, such as the prefrontal cortex, which is linked to attention and working memory, and the insula, which plays a role in emotional regulation and self-awareness. Another study examined the effects of an eight-week mindfulness meditation program on participants' brains. The research involved 68 healthy adults split into meditation and control groups. After the eight weeks, those in the meditation group exhibited increased activity in the anterior cingulate cortex, a brain area connected to cognitive control and emotion regulation. In a separate study focusing on people with generalized anxiety disorder, researchers observed the effects of a mindfulness-based stress reduction program on participants' brains. The findings revealed that after completing the program, there was enhanced connectivity between the default mode and executive control networks, which are involved in self-referential thinking and cognitive control, respectively. This increased connectivity could indicate better attentional control and decreased mind-wandering. These studies imply that regular meditation can result in brain changes contributing to an increased sense of mindfulness and presence. These alterations may be linked to improved attention, emotional regulation, and cognitive control.

At its core, meditation is the practice of cultivating mindfulness, or the ability to be fully present and aware of one's thoughts, feelings, and bodily sensations without judgment. By developing mindfulness, individuals can learn to observe their inner experiences with curiosity and compassion rather than becoming overwhelmed or consumed by them. This heightened self-awareness can lead to increased emotional regulation, improved mental health, and a greater sense of inner peace. While the techniques and objectives of meditation may vary, they all share a common goal: to train the mind to be more present, aware, and at peace with the ever-changing stream of thoughts, emotions, and experiences that make up our lives. By developing a regular meditation practice, individuals can experience numerous benefits, such as reduced stress, improved mental and emotional well-being, enhanced self-awareness, and a greater sense of connection to oneself and the world.

The beauty of meditation is that it's not about controlling your thoughts; it's about observing them without judgment. It's about becoming familiar with them and learning to let them go. Just as a surfer doesn't try to control the waves but instead learns to ride them, we can learn to ride the waves of our thoughts and emotions through meditation. By becoming familiar with our thoughts and emotions, we can let go of the ones that no longer serve us. We can create new neural pathways in our brains, rewire automatic responses, and become more present in our daily lives. This heightened awareness makes identifying emotional triggers and patterns easier, enabling individuals to better regulate their emotional responses to various situations.

There are several techniques that individuals can employ to cultivate presence and increase their ability to remain fully engaged in the present moment. These methods can be integrated into daily life and practiced regularly to enhance overall well-being and satisfaction. One effective technique for cultivating presence is focused attention meditation, which involves directing attention to a specific object, such as the breath, a mantra, or a bodily sensation. By continually returning attention to this focal point whenever the mind wanders, individuals can develop the ability to maintain focus on the present moment and become more aware of their internal experiences.

Body scanning is another valuable method for cultivating presence. This practice involves systematically directing one's attention to different parts of the body and observing any sensations that arise without judgment. By becoming more attuned to the body's physical sensations and the present-moment experience, individuals can enhance their awareness of the present moment and develop a greater connection to their physical selves. Mindful movement practices, such as yoga, tai chi, or qigong, can also help to cultivate presence. Another technique for cultivating presence is the practice of mindful listening. This practice involves fully engaging one's attention in listening without judgment or distraction. By focusing on the sounds and words being spoken, individuals can develop a greater sense of presence and improve their ability to communicate and connect with others.

Mindful eating is another opportunity to transcend the body

and become fully present in the moment. It is easy to get caught up in distractions while eating. Many people eat while watching television, scrolling through their smartphones, or working at their desks. This behavior can lead to mindless eating and a disconnection from the experience of enjoying our food. Mindful eating is an opportunity to break this pattern and bring our full attention to the act of eating. By focusing on the flavors, textures, and sensations of the food, we can become more mindful of our eating habits and experience the full pleasure of the meal. Eating mindfully can also help to be more aware of their bodies' hunger and fullness signals, promoting healthy eating habits.

Engaging in creative activities like drawing, painting, or writing can also help individuals transcend the body by bringing them into a flow state. In this state, individuals become fully immersed in the creative process and lose track of time and space. Individuals can let go of distractions and become more present in the moment. Finally, being in nature can help individuals transcend the body by connecting with the natural world and becoming fully present in the moment. The sights, sounds, and sensations of the outdoors can be a powerful reminder of the beauty and interconnectedness of all things. By spending time in nature, individuals can let go of distractions and cultivate inner peace and tranquility.

Transcending the Body, Environment, and time is a crucial aspect of meditation. It enables practitioners to move beyond the limitations imposed by their physical form and surroundings and gain a deeper understanding of their true nature. By transcending these boundaries, individuals can experience profound states of consciousness, inner peace, and personal growth. One of the primary goals of many meditation practices is to cultivate a sense of detachment from the body. This detachment allows individuals to shift their focus from the physical sensations and discomforts that may arise during meditation to the subtle movements of energy and consciousness within. As individuals become less identified with their physical form, they often experience greater freedom and expansiveness, enabling them to explore more profound levels of awareness and spiritual insight.

Similarly, meditation can help individuals transcend their environment by cultivating tranquility, regardless of external circumstances. Through consistent meditation, individuals can learn to remain centered and composed even in challenging situations, such as stress, adversity, or emotional turmoil. This ability to maintain inner balance and composure can profoundly impact one's ability to navigate the complexities of daily life with grace and resilience. Another aspect of transcending during meditation is the experience of moving beyond time constraints. As individuals delve deeper into meditation, they may discover that their perception of time begins to shift, with moments of deep meditation stretching for much longer than their actual duration. This altered sense of time can provide a glimpse into the timeless nature of consciousness, offering a profound understanding of the interconnectedness of all things and the eternal present moment.

Transcending the body, environment, and time during meditation can lead to numerous benefits, including enhanced self-awareness, increased clarity of mind, and a deeper sense of inner peace. By learning to move beyond the limitations of their physical form, individuals can gain valuable insights into the true nature of reality and their place within it. This expanded perspective can foster a greater sense of purpose, meaning, and fulfillment as individuals recognize all existence's inherent interconnectedness and unity. These activities encourage individuals to bring their full attention to the body, promoting a deep connection to the present moment. By engaging in these mindful practices, individuals can develop greater body awareness, improve physical health, and enhance their ability to remain present.

UNVEILING THE CONSCIOUS AND SUBCONSCIOUS MINDS THROUGH MEDITATION

We all have two minds working within us: the conscious and the subconscious. The conscious mind is the part of our mind that we use to process and analyze information. It allows us to make decisions, solve problems, and perform daily activities. It is the part of our mind that we are aware of and can actively control. On the other hand, the subconscious mind operates below the level of our conscious awareness. It is responsible for storing our memories, beliefs, and habits, and it influences our behavior in ways we may not even be aware of. The subconscious mind can be thought of as a sort of autopilot that guides our behavior based on past experiences and conditioning.

For example, let's say you have a fear of dogs that developed after a traumatic experience as a child. Even if you consciously know that most dogs are friendly and pose no threat to you, your subconscious mind may still trigger a fear response when you see a dog based on the past experience stored in your subconscious. Another example is the way we develop habits. We often perform specific actions or behaviors repeatedly until they become automatic and require little conscious thought. These habits are formed in the subconscious mind; once they are established, they can be difficult to change. Driving is another example of how the conscious and subconscious mind collaborate. At times, we can become so familiar with a route that we forget we are driving, and our subconscious mind takes over. We may arrive at our destination without recalling how we got there or any specific actions we took while driving. This is because our subconscious mind has stored the memories and habits of driving that particular route. The conscious mind, in this case, is free to focus on other tasks, such as daydreaming or planning for the day ahead.

Understanding the workings of the conscious and subconscious mind can be helpful in personal growth and self-improvement. By becoming more aware of our subconscious beliefs and habits, we can work to change them and create more positive patterns of behavior. But what happens when we want to change something in our lives? How can we tap into our subconscious mind to shift our thinking and behavior? This is where meditation comes into play.

Meditation has been shown to help lower the veil between our conscious and subconscious minds. By practicing meditation, we can slow down the constant chatter of our conscious mind and access the deeper layers of our being. This approach allows us to become aware of our automatic thoughts and behaviors that are often influenced by our subconscious mind.

The human body is an incredible machine that has the ability to repair and regenerate itself. The chemicals and energies released during the state of meditation help us to overcome stress and illness. As the mind becomes more focused and present, you may start to notice feelings of love and compassion to arise naturally. This process may involve directing feelings of love towards oneself, loved ones, strangers, or even difficult people. When we experience love, our body produces oxytocin, also known as the "cuddle hormone." Oxytocin promotes trust, connection, and well-being and has been shown to reduce stress and anxiety. In addition, it also has physical benefits such as reducing inflammation and promoting wound healing.

Joy and happiness are associated with the release of endorphins, which are natural painkillers that can also produce a sense of euphoria. Endorphins also help to reduce stress and anxiety. During meditation, the body may experience a sense of relaxation and calmness, which can help reduce stress hormone levels like cortisol and adrenaline. As the practice deepens, you may begin to experience a sense of detachment from your thoughts and emotions, which can lead to inner peace and happiness. This can trigger the release of endorphins, leading to a sense of euphoria or "runner's high."

Gratitude is a powerful emotion that has been shown to have numerous benefits on our physical and mental health. Studies have found that when we experience gratitude, our brain releases dopamine and serotonin, two neurotransmitters crucial in regulating mood and emotions. One study found that participants who practiced gratitude exercises showed increased activity in the brain's reward centers, which are associated with dopamine release. The study involved having participants write letters of gratitude to someone they were thankful for. The researchers found that this simple exercise led to increased feelings of gratitude and positive emotions. Another study explored gratitude's effects on serotonin levels in the brain. The study involved having participants practice a gratitude meditation, focusing on feelings of appreciation and gratitude towards themselves and others. The researchers found that participants showed increased serotonin levels after the meditation, which is known to regulate mood and emotions.

Dopamine is often called the "feel-good" chemical because it helps create a sense of pleasure and reward in the brain. At the same time, serotonin is associated with feelings of happiness and well-being. By increasing the levels of these neurotransmitters, gratitude can help to boost our mood and reduce symptoms of depression and anxiety. In addition to its effects on neurotransmitters, gratitude has also been shown to reduce inflammation in the body. Chronic inflammation has been linked to various health problems, including heart disease, diabetes, and cancer. By reducing inflammation, gratitude may help to protect against these conditions and promote overall health and longevity. Furthermore, research suggests that gratitude may promote the release of the hormone DHEA, which has been shown to have numerous benefits on our physical and mental health. DHEA helps to boost the immune system, improve brain function, and reduce the risk of age-related diseases such as osteoporosis and Alzheimer's. Trusting relationships and feelings of social support can also activate the release of DHEA, further emphasizing the importance of cultivating positive relationships in our lives.

When we are fully present, our body's energy field expands and becomes more coherent, meaning that the energy waves produced by the body become more synchronized and ordered. This coherence has been measured through heart rate variability and electroencephalogram (EEG) recordings. Research has shown that individuals who experience greater coherence in their energy field have a more resilient nervous system and are better able to handle stress. Researchers found that individuals who regularly practiced meditation had greater heart coherence and increased heart rate variability (HRV) compared to those who did not. This outcome suggests that regular meditation practice can help individuals cultivate a more balanced and resilient nervous system. One of the key factors in this coherence is the role of the heart. The heart produces a powerful electromagnetic field that can be measured up to several feet away from the body. When we experience positive emotions such as gratitude, love, and compassion, the heart's electromagnetic field becomes more coherent and harmonious, enhancing the coherence of the body's overall energy field.

Our minds expand, and we become less self-centered and

more selfless. We start to imagine a reality beyond our senses, looking at all the possibilities instead of just the limited ones. We crave the unknown because we know that it's the key to creating something new and unique in our lives. This shift in perspective is crucial in moving from simply surviving to living in creation. When we are in survival mode, we focus on our basic needs, our bodies, and the immediate threats around us. We are preoccupied with meeting physical and emotional needs such as food, shelter, and safety.

For example, a person struggling to make ends meet and pay rent may be entirely focused on working long hours and finding ways to make ends meet. This person may constantly be stressed and anxious about their financial situation, leading to a narrow perspective and limited decision-making abilities. However, when we live in creation, we open ourselves to the bigger picture and look beyond ourselves. We begin to see all the possibilities that exist and understand that we have the power to create something new and exciting. It involves setting goals and aspirations that allow us to grow and evolve. This shift in mindset is critical in moving us from a place of stress and anxiety to one of empowerment and possibility.

By cultivating these heartfelt emotions, we open ourselves up to a state of being that benefits not only our bodies but also our minds and souls. We become less focused on the stresses and worries of our lives and more attuned to the world around us. Our minds expand, and we start to see things in a different light. Suddenly, the unknown becomes an adventure, and we are excited to explore it. The connection between the mind and the body is incredibly deep and complex. It has been well-established that the mind can have a powerful impact on the body, but the relationship between the mind and the body is actually a two-way street - just as the mind can impact the body, the body can also impact the mind. This bidirectional relationship means that taking care of your physical health can positively impact your mental health and vice versa.

The body is not just a physical entity but also a mental and emotional entity. It is affected by negative emotions such as anger, sadness, envy, regret, guilt, and others. The level of harmony or disharmony in the mind affects how well the physical vehicle functions. Therefore, taking responsibility and becoming aware of the negativity one harbors inside is vital. Traditional medical practices have mostly ignored the connection between the mind and the body and have even denied its existence. However, it is evident that there is a connection, and if we are aware of it, we can use it to our advantage. A simple exercise in understanding the relationship between the mind and the body is to close your eyes and imagine biting into a lemon. You will immediately feel saliva accumulating in your mouth, even though there was no lemon, just the thought of it.

The mind may create physical problems to distract us from emotional pain. Often, emotional pain is not recognized or exists beneath the level of awareness. It can come out as certain kinds of reactivity in daily life. It is taken over by reactions to certain things that trigger emotional pain that is in you that you're completely unaware of, and emotional pain that is in total unawareness can very quickly become a physical symptom. It is essential to recognize that what goes on in the mind affects the body. Triggers can be anything that sets off an emotional response in us, and they can come in different forms. For instance, it could be a negative comment from a friend or a colleague, a reminder of a past traumatic event, a specific smell, or a situation that brings up unpleasant memories.

Triggers can also be subtle and unexpected, and they can cause different reactions in different people. It's essential to understand that while somebody else may have triggered us, we are responsible for our reactions. Our reactions are based on our thoughts, emotions, and past experiences, and we have the power to control them. We can choose to react positively, negatively, or not at all. By taking responsibility for our reactions, we can reduce the impact of triggers on our lives. One way to manage triggers is to get to know ourselves better. By understanding our emotional triggers and the reasons behind them, we can learn to identify and manage them more effectively.

In order to find an entry point into the practice of meditation, you will find an easy step-by-step meditation guide at the end of the book that you can use and adjust to your personal preferences.

COHERENCE
Chapter Eight

BRAIN COHERENCE AND BRAIN-HEART SYNCHRONIZATION

Brain coherence refers to the harmonious synchronization of neural oscillations within different regions of the brain. This synchronization plays a crucial role in efficiently exchanging information between various brain areas, allowing for optimal cognitive functioning, emotional regulation, and overall health. Recent research has also revealed the importance of brain-heart coherence, which involves synchronizing the brain's neural activity and the heart's rhythmic patterns. Coherence between these two vital systems can improve mental, emotional, and physical health. Conversely, a lack of coherence can negatively impact one's life, manifesting as cognitive difficulties, emotional imbalances, and stress-related health issues.

When the different parts of the brain work in coherence, information processing and transmission become more efficient. This improved communication allows for better problem-solving, decision-making, and memory consolidation. Individuals with high levels of brain coherence may also experience increased mental clarity, focus, and creativity, enabling them to excel in personal and professional settings. Coherence within the brain, particularly between the prefrontal cortex and the limbic system, facilitates effective emotional regulation. This balance allows individuals to better understand and manage their emotions and promoting resilience in life's challenges.

Brain coherence contributes to increased neuroplasticity, the brain's ability to adapt and reorganize its neural connections in response to new experiences and challenges. This heightened capacity for change supports learning and skill acquisition throughout one's life and the brain's ability to recover and rewire itself following injuries or other adverse events. Achieving coherence within the brain can reduce stress and anxiety levels, allowing for more effective communication between the brain's cognitive and emotional centers. This harmonious interaction enables individuals to respond more adaptively to stressors and manage anxiety more effectively, fostering a sense of calm and emotional stability.

Coherence between the prefrontal cortex and the hypothalamus is essential for maintaining healthy sleep patterns. This synchronization supports the proper functioning of the body's internal clock, or circadian rhythm, promoting restorative sleep and optimal daytime functioning. Research suggests that effective communication between different brain regions may help regulate the body's immune response, protecting against infections and inflammation and promoting overall physical health. When the different parts of the brain work coherently, individuals experience greater well-being and satisfaction with life. This harmonious state allows for better management of thoughts and emotions, leading to a more positive outlook, enhanced resilience, and stronger social connections.

In addition to brain coherence, the concept of brain-heart coherence has gained significant attention in recent years. This form of coherence is based on the understanding that the heart and the brain are interconnected and communicate with each other in a bidirectional manner. The heart sends signals to the brain through various pathways, including the nervous system, hormones, and electromagnetic fields. The brain, in turn, processes these signals and sends messages back to the heart, influencing its function. Achieving brain-heart coherence involves synchronizing the brain's neural oscillations with the heart's rhythmic patterns, creating harmony between these two systems. Research has shown that when the heart's rhythms are stable and consistent, the brain functions more efficiently, allowing for improved cognitive performance and emotional stability. This state of coherence has been linked to numerous health benefits, including reduced stress, enhanced immune function, and a lower risk of chronic disease.

Various practices can be employed to cultivate brain-heart coherence, such as mindfulness meditation, deep breathing exercises, and biofeedback. These techniques help to train the mind and body to work together harmoniously, promoting a state of coherence and fostering overall well-being. HeartMath, a research-based organization, has developed specific tools and techniques to help individuals achieve brain-heart coherence, which have been shown to improve mental, emotional, and physical health. On the other hand, a lack of brain-heart coherence can contribute to a range of negative consequences in one's life. Disrupted communication between the brain and the heart can lead to heightened stress levels, increased anxiety, and diminished emotional regulation. Additionally, chronic stress resulting from a lack of coherence can impair immune function, increase inflammation, and contribute to the development of chronic diseases such as cardiovascular disease, diabetes, and mental health disorders.

Achieving coherence within the different parts of the brain offers a multitude of benefits that can significantly enhance one's cognitive, emotional, and physical health. By cultivating practices that promote brain coherence, such as mindfulness meditation, deep breathing exercises, and engaging in mentally stimulating activities, individuals can tap into their brain's full potential and enjoy a richer, more fulfilling life. As research in this field continues to grow, we can expect a deeper understanding of the mechanisms underlying coherence and its potential applications for personal and professional development.

THE IMPORTANCE OF COHERENCE IN THOUGHTS AND EMOTIONS

When we achieve coherence, we unlock our full potential and access the power of the quantum field. This field, which permeates space and time, governs the behavior of particles and forces in the universe. Imagine a field that extends throughout space and time, with different types of particles having their own fields. Particles can be thought of as tiny waves or ripples in these fields, interacting with each other by exchanging energy. Quantum field theory helps us better understand how the building blocks of the universe work and interact, even when things get really small and the laws of traditional physics no longer apply. The significance of coherence in creating with the field cannot be overstated. Achieving coherence means establishing harmony between our thoughts and emotions and synchronizing our brain and heart functions. This harmony is essential for successfully accessing the quantum field and manifesting our intentions. When we are in a state of coherence, our thoughts and emotions work together, amplifying our creative abilities and allowing us to interact with the quantum field more effectively.

In a state of coherence, we become more attuned to our intuition, which guides our decision-making process and helps us navigate life with greater clarity. Our heightened intuition also enables us to perceive subtle cues from the quantum field, which provides valuable information that can aid us in our manifestation journey. Moreover, a coherent state allows us to experience a deeper connection with ourselves, others, and the universe, fostering a profound sense of belonging and unity. Coherence also directly impacts our mental, emotional, and physical health. When we are coherent, we experience less stress, anxiety, and negative emotions, promoting a healthy immune system, balanced hormonal levels, and overall vitality. This state of well-being enables us to maintain a high vibrational frequency, essential for attracting positive experiences and manifesting our desired reality. Achieving coherence is paramount in our quest to create with the field. It enhances our ability to manifest our desires and improves our intuition, and connection with the universe. By striving for coherence, we unlock our full potential and empower ourselves to shape our reality according to our intentions and aspirations.

Brain coherence is a critical aspect of creating with the field. It refers to the harmonious functioning and synchronization of various regions within the brain, allowing for optimal communication between different neural networks. When our brain operates in a coherent state, it becomes more efficient, adaptive, and responsive to internal and external stimuli. During brain coherence, several distinct yet interconnected processes occur within the brain, involving various regions and networks. These processes work together to create a harmonious state that enhances cognitive function, emotional regulation, and overall mental health. Let's take a closer look at what happens in different parts of the brain during brain coherence.

Prefrontal Cortex

The prefrontal cortex, located at the front of the brain, is responsible for executive functions such as decision-making, problem-solving, and emotional regulation. The prefrontal cortex operates more efficiently during brain coherence, allowing for better impulse control, focused attention, and enhanced cognitive flexibility. This improved functioning of the prefrontal cortex enables us to respond more adaptively to various situations rather than relying on habitual patterns and reactions.

Amygdala

The amygdala, a small almond-shaped structure deep within the brain, plays a crucial role in processing emotions, particularly fear and anxiety. When brain coherence is achieved, the amygdala becomes less reactive to stressful stimuli, which reduces feelings of fear and anxiety. This reduced reactivity allows for better emotional regulation and resilience to stress.

Hippocampus

The hippocampus is a key structure for learning and memory formation. During brain coherence, the hippocampus becomes more active, facilitating the consolidation of new information and the retrieval of stored memories. This heightened activity supports learning, creativity, and problem-solving abilities.

Corpus Callosum

The corpus callosum is a thick band of nerve fibers connecting the brain's left and right hemispheres, facilitating communication between them. In a state of brain coherence, the corpus callosum enables more effective integration of information between the hemispheres, leading to better cognitive functioning and enhanced creativity.

Thalamus

The thalamus acts as a relay station for sensory information, transmitting signals to the appropriate areas of the brain for further processing. During brain coherence, the thalamus functions more efficiently, allowing for improved sensory integration and a heightened awareness of our surroundings.

Default Mode Network (DMN)

The DMN is a network of brain regions that become active when the mind is at rest, such as during daydreaming or self-referential thinking. In a coherent brain state, the activity of the DMN is reduced, leading to a decrease in self-focused rumination and increased present-moment awareness.

Brain coherence is vital in creating with the field because it allows us to access higher states of consciousness and tap into the quantum field more effectively. A coherent brain is better equipped to receive and interpret information from the field, enabling us to align our intentions with our actions and manifest our desires more efficiently. Furthermore, brain coherence allows us to cultivate a deeper sense of self-awareness, which is crucial for identifying and overcoming limiting beliefs and patterns that may hinder our manifestation process. By understanding and implementing techniques to cultivate coherence, individuals can experience a range of benefits, leading to improved mental, emotional, and physical well-being.

THE NEGATIVE IMPACT ON SOCIETY FROM LACK OF BRAIN COHERENCE

In today's fast-paced and highly connected world, many factors contribute to a lack of brain coherence in individuals, which has a collective impact on society as a whole. This lack of brain coherence can manifest as increased stress levels, heightened anxiety, poor emotional regulation, and a decline in cognitive functioning. As a result, it affects various aspects of life, including mental health, interpersonal relationships and productivity.

The proliferation of technology, particularly smartphones and social media, has given rise to endless connectivity and a constant flood of information. The brain can become overwhelmed by this continuous stream of stimuli, resulting in diminished coherence and focus. Moreover, the addictive nature of social media platforms, coupled with the inclination to compare oneself to others, fosters feelings of inadequacy, anxiety, and depression. This has led to a vicious cycle where individuals seek validation through likes and shares, further exacerbating mental health issues and negatively impacting overall well-being. The relentless demands of contemporary life frequently necessitate multitasking and managing multiple responsibilities simultaneously. Although this approach might appear efficient in terms of time management, it can actually hinder brain coherence by compelling the brain to rapidly switch between tasks. This fragmented attention can lead to a decline in focus, weakened memory retention, and a decrease in overall productivity. Consequently, the quality of work and personal life suffers, creating a cycle of stress and inefficiency.

In today's society, individuals often find it challenging to remain present and mindful, becoming preoccupied with concerns about the future or dwelling on past events. This absence of present-moment awareness disrupts brain coherence, as the brain becomes consumed by thoughts and emotions unrelated to the immediate task. This disharmony can result in reduced mental clarity, suboptimal decision-making, and a decline in emotional well-being, ultimately affecting personal and professional relationships and individual satisfaction and happiness. The increasing prevalence of anxiety, depression, and other mental health disorders highlights the detrimental impact of a lack of brain coherence on individuals. This growing mental health crisis affects not only personal well-being but also places considerable strain on healthcare systems and society at large. As mental health issues become more widespread, the demand for mental health services, support, and resources continues to grow, putting pressure on already overwhelmed systems and increasing the need for prevention and early intervention strategies.

The inability to regulate emotions effectively and maintain focus can hamper individuals' capacity to communicate and forge meaningful connections with others. This can lead to tension in relationships, heightened conflict, and a deterioration in social cohesion. As communication and emotional intelligence suffer, individuals may feel isolated, disconnected, and misunderstood, further contributing to the decline in mental health and social harmony. When individuals are overwhelmed by stress and emotional distress, cultivating empathy and compassion for others becomes a significant challenge. This erosion of empathy may contribute to social divisions, heightened conflict, and a decline in collective well-being. A society with reduced empathy and compassion is more prone to misunderstandings, intolerance, and disconnection, leading to an environment where personal and societal well-being suffers. This creates a further barrier to fostering empathy and compassion, perpetuating the cycle of disconnection and discontent.

THE LIMITATIONS OF SENSORY PERCEPTION

Our sensory organs, ingeniously designed for survival, gather information about our immediate surroundings to help us navigate daily life. However, these senses only offer a narrow glimpse of reality, filtering out an enormous expanse of information beyond our perceptual grasp. Our senses are intrinsically biased, prioritizing aspects of our environment that directly impact our survival, shaping our unique perception of the world.

For example, we can only see a tiny portion of the electromagnetic spectrum specifically visible light (Figure 5), leaving the vast majority of the spectrum, including radio waves, microwaves, and X-rays, undetected. This is akin to observing a colossal, intricate painting but only being able to perceive a few brushstrokes. Similarly, our auditory range is limited, as we cannot hear the ultrasonic communication of bats or the subsonic frequencies of elephants. This would be like listening to a grand symphony but only hearing a few select instruments. Moreover, our sense of smell pales compared to a bloodhound, which can detect scents up to 100 million times more effectively. Even our taste buds are confined, with only five basic tastes that we can discern, while other creatures, such as the catfish, can taste thousands of distinct flavors. Our tactile sense is similarly constrained, as we are unable to perceive the faint air currents detected by the sensitive whiskers of a cat.

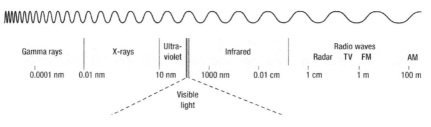

Figure 5: The Visible Light Spectrum.

These examples highlight our narrow perceptual window into reality as we experience a world tailored to our needs and perspectives rather than an objective, all-encompassing truth.

Consequently, it is essential to recognize the limitations of our senses and seek a deeper understanding of the vast universe that lies hidden beyond our immediate sensory experiences. Furthermore, our senses are susceptible to deception, resulting in illusions, misconceptions, and a skewed comprehension of our surroundings. Optical illusions are prime examples of how our visual perception can be duped into perceiving nonexistent elements or misinterpreting the spatial relationships between objects. Our senses can act as unreliable narrators, feeding us distorted information that shapes our understanding of the world.

For example, the famous Müller-Lyer illusion, where two lines of equal length appear different due to arrow-like endings (Figure 6), highlights how visual context can easily deceive our brains. Similarly, auditory illusions, such as the Shepard Tone, create the impression of a never-ending ascending or descending pitch, despite the fact that the sound is cyclic and finite.

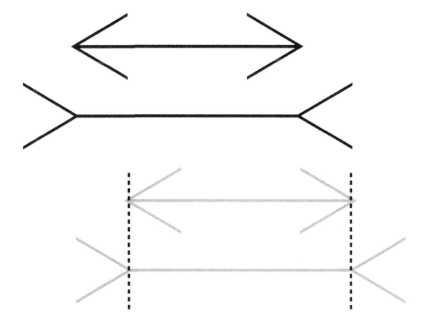

Figure 6: Müller-Lyer Optical Illusion.

Plato's Allegory of the Cave is a fitting metaphor to illustrate our sensory limitations and the deceptive nature of our perceptions. In the allegory, prisoners chained inside a cave can only see the shadows of objects cast on the cave wall, leading them to believe that the shadows are the entirety of reality. When a prisoner is finally freed and exposed to the outside world, he discovers that the shadows were mere illusions and that reality extends far beyond his initial understanding. Similarly, we are the metaphorical prisoners in our own perceptual cave, limited by the confines of our senses and prone to deception.

Figure 7: Plato's Allegory of the Cave.

Given these limitations, it becomes apparent that relying solely on our sensory perception can hinder our ability to comprehend the nature of reality fully. To gain a more accurate and comprehensive understanding, we must recognize the constraints of our senses and seek alternative ways to access information beyond the realm of our immediate sensory experience. By doing so, we can explore the true nature of reality, transcending the limitations imposed by our senses and unlocking a deeper, more profound understanding of the world and our place within it.

Our five senses provide us with a restricted understanding of the world, confining us within the parameters of our immediate environment. However, there are ways to transcend these boundaries and access a more profound comprehension of existence. One approach to transcending space-time is by exploring our consciousness, which is not bound by the same limitations as our physical bodies. By developing a deeper understanding of our inner selves and the nature of consciousness, we can experience a sense of interconnectedness with the universe, going beyond the constraints of our physical reality. In the course of history, various individuals have claimed to transcend space-time and gain knowledge otherwise unattainable through conventional means. These experiences have shaped their lives and contributed to the collective human understanding of the nature of reality. Some notable examples include:

Edgar Cayce

Edgar Cayce was born on March 18, 1877, in Hopkinsville, Kentucky, and grew up in a devout Christian family. From an early age, he displayed psychic abilities and extraordinary sensitivities, including seeing auras and communicating with the deceased. Despite his initial reluctance to accept these abilities, Cayce eventually came to terms with his gift and began providing psychic readings in his adult life. Cayce's journey toward transcending space-time began in earnest when he started giving readings in a self-induced hypnotic trance state. During these trances, he was able to access a vast storehouse of knowledge known as the "Akashic Records," which contained information on every soul's past, present, and future. It was as if he could travel beyond the constraints of time and space to retrieve information that would have otherwise remained hidden from human perception. Throughout his life, Cayce provided more than 14,000 documented readings on various topics, including health, past lives, and future events. Many of these readings were later validated by independent researchers and experts in their respective fields. His work in health showcased a deep understanding of the human body and offered innovative treatments for various ailments, some of which were far ahead of their time. Cayce's ability to transcend space-time allowed him to bring forth groundbreaking insights into the nature of reality, human consciousness, and our connection to the universe. His readings covered a wide range of subjects, such as ancient civilizations, the origin and purpose of the soul, the existence of extraterrestrial life, and the interplay between spiritual and physical realms. Edgar Cayce's legacy has endured, and his contributions to metaphysics, spirituality, and alternative medicine continue to inspire and influence countless individuals worldwide. His life's journey is a testament to the potential for transcending space-time and accessing the hidden realms of knowledge that lie beyond our ordinary sensory perception.

Nikola Tesla

Nikola Tesla was born on July 10, 1856, in the small village of Smiljan in modern-day Croatia. He was a brilliant inventor, physicist, and electrical engineer whose numerous groundbreaking discoveries and inventions revolutionized the world of electrical technology. With more than 300 patents, Tesla's innovations laid the foundation for modern wireless communication, alternating current (AC) power systems, and many other technologies that have since become integral to our daily lives. Tesla's journey towards transcending space-time can be traced back to his unique mental abilities and thought processes. He possessed an extraordinary capacity for visualizing complex ideas and inventions in his mind's eye, which allowed him to design, test, and perfect his creations entirely within his imagination before bringing them into the physical world. This ability, often referred to as "thought experiments" or "mental simulations," enabled Tesla to access a realm beyond the constraints of space and time, where he could freely explore and manipulate the fundamental principles that govern the universe. Throughout his life, Tesla maintained that his ideas and inventions were inspired by an intuitive connection to a universal source of knowledge, which he believed transcended the boundaries of ordinary human experience. He often spoke of receiving flashes of insight during periods of intense focus or contemplation, which he claimed provided him with access to information and ideas that were far beyond the scope of his prior knowledge and experience. Tesla's dedication to harnessing the unseen forces of nature and his unwavering belief in the power of human consciousness to transcend space-time led him to explore groundbreaking concepts such as wireless energy transmission, the potential for global communication systems, and even the possibility of tapping into the Earth's natural resonant frequencies for unlimited power. While many of his more ambitious ideas were met with skepticism during his time, they have since inspired generations of scientists and inventors to push the boundaries of what is deemed possible in our understanding of the universe. Nikola Tesla's life and work serve as a powerful reminder of the potential within the human mind to access and harness the vast reservoir of knowledge beyond the limits of our sensory perception. His extraordinary ability to transcend space-time and envision the possibilities of a technologically advanced future has left a lasting impact on the world and continues to inspire countless individuals to explore the outer reaches of human potential.

Hildegard of Bingen

Hildegard of Bingen was born on September 16, 1098, in Bermersheim vor der Höhe, a small village in present-day Germany. She was a Benedictine abbess, mystic, composer, and polymath who made significant contributions to theology, medicine, and the arts during the Middle Ages. Hildegard was an influential figure within the church and the wider world. Her remarkable body of work and spiritual insights continue to inspire and inform contemporary scholars, artists, and spiritual seekers alike. Hildegard's journey towards transcending space-time began at a very young age when she started experiencing vivid visions and mystical experiences that seemed to defy the ordinary bounds of human perception. These visions, which Hildegard described as "the reflection of the Living

Light," provided her with access to an extraordinary wealth of knowledge, wisdom, and creative inspiration that guided her throughout her life. Hildegard believed that her ability to transcend space-time and access this divine source of knowledge was a gift from God. She devoted her life to sharing her insights and revelations with others through her writings, teachings, and creative works. Among her most notable achievements are her theological texts, such as "Scivias," "Liber Vitae Meritorum," and "Liber Divinorum Operum," which detail her visionary experiences and provide a comprehensive account of her unique understanding of the cosmos, human nature, and the divine. In addition to her theological works, Hildegard made significant contributions to medicine and natural science, composing an extensive compendium of herbal remedies and treatments known as "Physica" and "Causae et Curae." These texts demonstrate her deep understanding of the natural world and the intricate connections between the human body, the environment, and the cosmos, which she believed were all governed by the same divine principles. As a composer, Hildegard created a vast collection of sacred music, including the hauntingly beautiful "Ordo Virtutum," a liturgical drama that is considered one of the earliest examples of its kind. Her music is characterized by its ethereal, transcendent quality, which evokes the timeless, otherworldly realm from which her inspiration was drawn. Hildegard of Bingen's life and work stand as a testament to the power of the human spirit to transcend the boundaries of space-time and access the hidden realms of knowledge and wisdom that lie beyond the reach of our everyday sensory experience. Her profound insights, mystical visions, and creative genius have left an indelible mark on the history of Western thought and continue to captivate and inspire individuals from all walks of life.

Ancient shamans and mystics

Ancient shamans and mystics have long been associated with the ability to transcend space-time, journeying beyond the confines of the physical world to access hidden realms of knowledge and wisdom. These spiritual practitioners, who have been present in virtually every culture and civilization throughout human history, are known for their unique capacity to enter altered states of consciousness and navigate the mysterious landscapes of the spirit world. The journey of ancient shamans and mystics towards transcending space-time often began with rigorous training and initiation, typically involving years of study and practice under the guidance of an experienced mentor. This preparation was necessary to develop the mental, emotional, and spiritual fortitude required to undertake the perilous journey into the unseen realms and return safely with the knowledge and insights they sought. A key component of the shamanic and mystical practice involved using various techniques and rituals to induce altered states of consciousness. These methods include meditation, fasting, sensory deprivation, rhythmic drumming, dance, and ingesting sacred plants or other psychoactive substances. By engaging in these practices, shamans and mystics could quiet their minds, tune out the distractions of the physical world, and enter a state of deep receptivity and communion with the spirit realm. Once they had successfully transcended the limitations of space-time, these spiritual practitioners would encounter various entities, spirits, and otherworldly beings who served as guides, teachers, and allies on their journey. Through these encounters, shamans and mystics were able to glean valuable insights and wisdom that could be applied to the healing and well-being of their communities, as well as to gain a greater understanding of the underlying patterns and principles that govern the cosmos. The experiences of ancient shamans and mystics, as well as the rich body of knowledge and wisdom they brought forth, provide a fascinating glimpse into the potential of the human spirit to transcend the boundaries of space-time and explore the vast, mysterious depths of existence. Their stories remind us that there is much more to reality than what meets the eye and that by tapping into our innate capacity for spiritual exploration and growth, we can access realms of knowledge and understanding that lie far beyond the reach of our ordinary senses.

These examples illustrate the potential for transcending space-time through various means, including meditation, trance states, and altered states of consciousness. By tapping into this expanded awareness, these individuals were able to access information and insights that would have been otherwise unattainable through conventional sensory perception, enriching human understanding of the nature of reality and our place within it.

THE REALM OF TIME-SPACE

Time-space is a theoretical construct that offers a different perspective on the nature of reality, allowing us to view the universe and our existence from a more expansive and interconnected vantage point. By understanding the principles and characteristics of time-space, we can begin to grasp the broader implications of our role in the cosmos and the profound potential that lies within each of us to shape our reality. In the realm of time-space, the linear progression of time that we typically perceive becomes malleable and less rigid, enabling a more fluid and holistic understanding of the temporal dimension.

Past, present, and future are not separate entities but rather interconnected aspects of a single, unified continuum. This perspective allows for the possibility of experiencing the entirety of one's life in a non-linear fashion, opening up the potential for accessing memories and insights from both past and future moments and understanding the intricate web of causality that connects all events and experiences.

Spatially, the realm of time-space also challenges our conventional understanding of distance and separation. In this dimension, space is not an absolute measure but is instead defined by relationships and interconnectedness. This concept implies that objects and entities in time-space are not isolated from one another but are rather intrinsically connected, regardless of the apparent physical distance between them. Consequently, the boundaries that we perceive between ourselves and the world around us begin to dissolve, revealing the underlying unity and oneness that permeates all of existence. Exploring the realm of time-space offers a unique opportunity to deepen our understanding of reality's true nature and human consciousness's vast potential. By transcending the limitations of our ordinary sensory perceptions and embracing a more holistic and interconnected view of the universe, we can access the hidden dimensions of existence and unlock the immense creative power within each of us.

Numerous individuals in history have contributed to developing and understanding the realm of time-space. Their insights, theories, and discoveries have helped to shape our current understanding of this fascinating dimension of reality. The most notable individuals include:

Albert Einstein

Albert Einstein, born on March 14, 1879, in Ulm, Germany, is widely recognized as one of the most influential physicists of the

20th century. From an early age, Einstein displayed a keen interest in mathematics and the natural sciences. He initially struggled in school due to his non-conformist thinking and the fixed educational system of the time. However, his curiosity and aptitude for understanding complex concepts led him to pursue a career in physics. Einstein's journey in contributing to developing the concept of time-space began with his groundbreaking work on the theory of relativity. In 1905, he published his special theory of relativity, which redefined the relationship between space and time. This theory established that space and time are not separate entities but are interwoven into a single, four-dimensional fabric known as space-time. According to the special theory of relativity, time and space are relative, meaning they depend on the observer's frame of reference. The speed of light is the same for all observers, regardless of their relative motion. In 1915, Einstein extended his special theory of relativity to include the effects of gravity, resulting in the general theory of relativity. This theory described gravity as a curvature of space-time caused by mass, leading to the prediction of phenomena such as the bending of light by massive objects and the expansion of the universe. Einstein's general theory of relativity has since been confirmed by various experiments and observations, solidifying its status as a cornerstone of modern physics. Einstein's work on the theory of relativity revolutionized our understanding of space and time and opened the door for further exploration of the realm of time-space. His theories challenged the classical notion of absolute space and time, which had dominated scientific thought since the days of Isaac Newton. By suggesting that space and time are interconnected and malleable, Einstein laid the groundwork for a new understanding of reality that transcends the limitations of our everyday experiences. Throughout his life, Einstein continued to explore the nature of space-time and its implications for our understanding of the cosmos. His work inspired generations of physicists and thinkers, paving the way for groundbreaking discoveries in cosmology, quantum mechanics, and the study of black holes. Albert Einstein's life and journey contributed to the creation of the concept of the realm of time-space and fundamentally transformed how we perceive and understand the universe.

John Archibald Wheeler

John Archibald Wheeler, born on July 9, 1911, in Jacksonville, Florida, was a prominent American theoretical physicist who made significant contributions to general relativity, quantum mechanics, and nuclear physics. Wheeler's early education was heavily influenced by his father, who was a librarian and encouraged his son's intellectual curiosity. He earned his Ph.D. from Johns Hopkins University in 1933 under the guidance of the renowned physicist Karl Herzfeld. Wheeler's work on the concept of time-space began during his collaboration with Albert Einstein in the 1930s. Wheeler and Einstein worked together at the Institute for Advanced Study in Princeton, where they further developed the general theory of relativity. They explored the implications of the theory in a variety of contexts, including the behavior of matter and radiation near extremely dense objects like black holes. Wheeler's most notable contribution to the realm of time-space was his work on the geometrodynamics of space-time. He developed the concept of "space-time foam," which posits that at the Planck scale, space-time undergoes constant fluctuations, creating a foam-like structure. This concept links general relativity and quantum mechanics, suggesting that the fabric of space-time is not smooth but rather a dynamic, ever-changing landscape influenced by quantum processes. In addition to his work on time-space, Wheeler was a pioneer in nuclear physics and played a crucial role in developing the atomic bomb during World War II. He also contributed significantly to the field of quantum mechanics, particularly in the area of quantum information theory. One of his most famous ideas, the "delayed-choice experiment," challenges our understanding of causality and highlights the fundamental role of the observer in the quantum realm. Throughout his career, John Archibald Wheeler mentored many students who became leading figures in physics, including Richard Feynman and Kip Thorne. He was known for effectively communicating complex scientific ideas and his passion for teaching. His work on time-space and other areas of physics has had a lasting impact on our understanding of the universe. His legacy continues to inspire future generations of physicists and thinkers.

David Bohm

David Bohm, born on December 20, 1917, in Wilkes-Barre, Pennsylvania, was a renowned theoretical physicist and philosopher who made substantial contributions to the understanding of quantum mechanics and the nature of reality. Bohm studied physics at Pennsylvania State University and later pursued his Ph.D. under the guidance of Robert Oppenheimer at the University of California, Berkeley. Despite facing significant challenges due to his political beliefs during the McCarthy era, Bohm persevered and established himself as a leading figure in the world of physics. Bohm's work on the concept of time-space emerged from his deep dissatisfaction with the orthodox interpretation of quantum mechanics, particularly its implications for the nature of reality. He felt that the prevalent Copenhagen interpretation, which posited an essential discontinuity between the observer and the observed, left many questions unanswered and could not account for the interconnectedness of all things. Bohm proposed a radical alternative to the Copenhagen interpretation: the "implicate order," which was based on the notion that the universe is a deeply interconnected, unbroken, and flowing whole. In this framework, time and space are not separate, independent entities but aspects of a more fundamental reality that unfolds and enfolds within itself. The implicate order implies that seemingly separate objects and events in our universe are deeply interconnected in a higher dimensional space-time. Bohm's ideas about the realm of time-space were further developed in collaboration with the Indian philosopher Jiddu Krishnamurti, with whom he shared a mutual interest in understanding the nature of reality and consciousness. Their dialogues led to the development of the "holomovement" concept, which suggests that reality is a constantly changing, unbroken flow of information and energy. Throughout his career, David Bohm's work on time-space, quantum mechanics, and the nature of reality has profoundly influenced physics and philosophy. His ideas continue to inspire researchers and thinkers across various disciplines, challenging conventional notions of space, time, and the nature of reality itself. Bohm's contributions to our understanding of the realm of time-space have left a lasting impact and continue to shape our perception of the universe and our place within it.

Carl Gustav Jung

Carl Gustav Jung, born on July 26, 1875, in Kesswil, Switzerland, was a pioneering psychiatrist and psychoanalyst who made significant contributions to the understanding of the human psyche and the nature of reality. Jung initially studied medicine at the University of Basel and later focused on psychiatry at the University of Zurich. He gained prominence through his collaboration with Sigmund Freud, which eventually ended due to their differing views on the nature of the unconscious mind. Jung's work on the concept of time-space was influenced by his exploration of the human psyche and his fascination with the relationship between consciousness, the unconscious mind, and the nature of reality. He sought to understand the deeper patterns and structures underlying human behavior, thoughts, and emotions. This led him to develop the concept of the "collective unconscious," a shared psychic structure that transcends individual consciousness and encompasses the archetypal patterns that inform human experience across cultures and throughout history. While not a physicist, Jung's contributions to our understanding of the realm of time-space were mainly his work on synchronicity, a concept he developed in collaboration with the physicist Wolfgang Pauli. Synchronicity refers to the meaningful coincidence of events connected beyond the bounds of ordinary causality. This idea challenges the conventional understanding of time and space, suggesting that seemingly separate events in the physical world can be deeply interconnected on a more fundamental level. Jung believed synchronicity reflected the underlying unity of the psyche and the physical world, a notion that resonated with the emerging ideas in quantum physics at the time. This concept has had a lasting impact on our understanding of the interconnectedness of the universe and the potential connections between consciousness and the fabric of reality. Carl Jung's work on the collective unconscious, archetypes, and synchronicity has profoundly influenced psychology, philosophy, and our understanding of reality. His ideas continue to inspire researchers and thinkers across various disciplines, challenging conventional notions of time, space, and the nature of human experience. Jung's contributions to our understanding of the realm of time-space have left a lasting impact and continue to shape our perception of the universe and our place within it.

Rupert Sheldrake

Rupert Sheldrake, born on June 28, 1942, in Newark-on-Trent,

England, is a renowned biologist, author, and researcher known for his groundbreaking work on the nature of consciousness, the interconnectedness of life, and the realm of time-space. Sheldrake studied biochemistry at the University of Cambridge and later pursued a Ph.D. in biochemistry from the same institution, focusing on plant development. Following his formal education, he conducted research at the University of Cambridge, the University of Malaya, and the Salk Institute in California, among other prestigious institutions. Sheldrake's most significant contribution to understanding time-space is his theory of "morphic resonance," which he introduced in his 1981 book "A New Science of Life." Morphic resonance posits that the forms and patterns of the physical world, including biological systems, are organized and influenced by non-local, invisible fields called "morphic fields." According to Sheldrake, these fields contain the collective memory and information of all past organisms and systems, connecting them through time and space. This concept challenges conventional scientific understanding, as it suggests that memory and information are not solely stored within the physical structures of organisms but are also held in these invisible, non-material fields. Sheldrake's ideas resonate with the emerging understanding of quantum entanglement and non-locality in physics, implying that there may be deeper connections between consciousness, biological systems, and the fabric of the universe. Rupert Sheldrake has also explored the nature of consciousness and its potential influence on the physical world through his research on telepathy, precognition, and other psychic phenomena. These studies further support the notion that the realm of time-space may be deeply interconnected with the workings of the human mind and the nature of reality itself. Sheldrake's work on morphic resonance and the interconnectedness of life has dramatically advanced our understanding of the realm of time-space and the fundamental principles that govern the universe. His ideas continue to inspire researchers and thinkers across various disciplines, offering new perspectives on the nature of reality and the potential connections between consciousness, biology, and the cosmos.

These individuals, along with many others, have played a crucial role in the development of the concept of the realm of time-space. Through their work, they have expanded our understanding of the nature of reality and the potential that exists within the vast, interconnected web of existence that transcends the boundaries of our everyday perception. Each of these concepts contributes to our understanding of the wholeness of existence, emphasizing the intrinsic interconnectedness of all elements within the intricate tapestry of reality. To truly understand this idea, we must first acknowledge that our linear perception of time and individualized sense of self may limit our ability to perceive the fundamental unity underlying all creation. By exploring various scientific, philosophical, and spiritual perspectives, we begin to uncover the profound implications of this interconnectedness for our understanding of the cosmos and our place within it.

The wholeness of existence is supported by a myriad of theories and discoveries in quantum physics, such as quantum entanglement and non-locality, which suggest that seemingly separate particles can be instantaneously connected regardless of the distance between them. Additionally, the holographic principle posits that the entire universe can be seen as a vast, interconnected web of information, where each part contains the information of the whole. Throughout history, philosophical and spiritual traditions from around the world have sought to understand and express the concept of the wholeness of existence, often emphasizing the deep interconnectedness and unity of all things. Two such traditions that provide invaluable insight into this concept are the Vedantic philosophy of India and the Buddhist concept of interdependence. Vedantic philosophy is rooted in the ancient Hindu scriptures known as the Vedas, which contain some of the oldest spiritual texts in human history. Central to Vedanta is the concept of Brahman, the ultimate reality that underlies and permeates all of existence. According to Vedanta, Brahman is the unchanging, eternal essence that constitutes the foundation of the universe, and everything in the cosmos is a manifestation of this singular, divine reality. This understanding of Brahman implies that all things, including our individual selves, are intrinsically connected and united at the deepest level of existence. Recognizing and experiencing this oneness with Brahman is considered the ultimate goal of spiritual practice in Vedanta. It leads to liberation from the illusion of separateness and the realization of our true nature as infinite and divine.

On the other hand, Buddhism strongly emphasizes the interconnected nature of all phenomena through the concept of interdependence or dependent origination. This principle posits that nothing exists in isolation, as all things arise and depend upon a complex web of causes and conditions. The Buddhist understanding of interdependence goes beyond mere physical connections, extending to the realms of thoughts, emotions, and actions. The teachings assert that our suffering and happiness are deeply intertwined with the suffering and happiness of others and that our actions have far-reaching consequences that reverberate throughout the interconnected web of existence. Both Vedantic philosophy and Buddhist teachings on interdependence share a profound insight into the wholeness of existence, emphasizing the interconnectedness of all things and the unity that underlies the apparent diversity of the cosmos.

By grasping the notion of the wholeness of existence, we recognize that our individual lives are intimately connected to the larger cosmic tapestry. This understanding can shift our perspective on our place in the universe and transform how we relate to ourselves, others, and the world around us. It invites us to cultivate greater compassion, empathy, and cooperation as we recognize that our actions have far-reaching consequences, impacting our personal lives and the broader web of existence. The realization of the wholeness of existence transforms our perspective on our place in the universe and prepares us for a deeper understanding of the concept of oneness. By acknowledging the intricate interconnectedness of all things, we lay the groundwork for perceiving oneness, a state where individual identities and boundaries dissolve, giving way to a unified whole. The perception of oneness is a profound realization that all living beings, objects, and phenomena in the universe are intrinsically interconnected and interdependent. This recognition transcends the boundaries of our identities and ego, allowing us to perceive ourselves as part of a unified whole rather than separate entities. By understanding the concept of oneness, we can begin to appreciate the deep relationships between ourselves, others, and the environment and the delicate balance that sustains life on Earth.

THE QUANTUM MIND
Chapter Nine

THE CONCEPT OF THE QUANTUM MIND

The concept of the quantum mind explores the potential intersection between quantum physics and consciousness, suggesting that our thoughts and emotions might influence the physical world on a quantum level. Quantum physics, a branch of physics that studies the behavior of particles at the subatomic level, has introduced several groundbreaking concepts, such as quantum entanglement and superposition. These phenomena challenge our traditional understanding of the physical world and have led some researchers to propose that quantum processes play a role in the nature of consciousness and the mind. The quantum mind hypothesis suggests that the mind and consciousness are not purely classical phenomena but rather be influenced by or even based on quantum processes occurring within the brain. There are several theories that propose a link between quantum processes and consciousness:

Quantum Holography theory, proposed by neuroscientist Karl Pribram, posits that the brain functions as a holographic storage system, with quantum processes playing a role in memory and cognition. According to this theory, memories and cognitive processes are not localized within specific regions of the brain; instead, they are distributed throughout the entire brain in a holographic manner. Think of the brain as a holographic storage system, like a 3D image produced by a laser. The entire image can be reconstructed from any part of the pattern in a hologram. Quantum Holography theory proposes that our memories and thoughts are similarly stored throughout the entire brain as holographic patterns formed by the interaction of brain waves. Quantum mechanics helps to explain how these patterns are created and accessed. The holographic principle suggests that information can be stored in a distributed pattern and that the whole can be reconstructed from any part of the pattern. In the context of the brain, this means that memories and cognitive processes are stored as interference patterns formed by the interaction of coherent waves generated by neural activity. Pribram's theory incorporates the principles of quantum mechanics, such as superposition and entanglement, to explain how these holographic interference patterns are formed and accessed.

The Quantum Field Theory of Consciousness, developed by molecular biologist Johnjoe McFadden, suggests that consciousness arises from the interaction of the brain's electromagnetic field with quantum processes occurring within neurons. According to this theory, the brain's electromagnetic field, generated by the electric currents produced by neurons, acts as a unifying force that integrates information from different brain regions, giving rise to conscious experience. Picture the brain as a busy city with a network of roads (neurons) and traffic (electric currents). The Quantum Field Theory of Consciousness suggests that the city's traffic patterns (the brain's electromagnetic field) interact with the roads (quantum processes in neurons) to create a unified experience of the city (consciousness). This theory explains how different aspects of our conscious perception come together coherently. McFadden's theory proposes that the brain's electromagnetic field interacts with quantum processes occurring within neurons, such as electron tunneling and ion channel activity. These interactions create an electromagnetic field pattern that encodes conscious experience.

The Quantum Field Theory of Consciousness aims to provide a unifying explanation for various aspects of consciousness, such as the binding problem, which refers to the integration of different sensory inputs into a unified conscious perception. The quantum mind hypothesis could have profound implications for understanding the power of the placebo effect and the mind-body connection. Our thoughts and emotions could influence the physical world on a quantum level, which helps explain how our beliefs, expectations, and attitudes can impact our physiological processes and overall health.

THE QUANTUM FIELD AND HUMAN CONSCIOUSNESS

The quantum field is an all-encompassing, underlying reality that connects everything in the universe. It consists of fluctuating energy and potentialities that give rise to the physical world as we know it. At the quantum level, particles and forces constantly interact, forming the building blocks of our reality. Imagine the quantum field as a vast, cosmic web connecting all the universe's stars, planets, and living beings. This web is woven from the threads of energy and potential that form the fabric of our reality. Each strand vibrates and interacts with the others, creating a dynamic tapestry of interconnectedness.

Human consciousness plays a critical role in interacting with the quantum field. Our thoughts, emotions, and intentions have the power to shape the field and, consequently, our reality. This idea is rooted in the observer effect, a concept in quantum mechanics that suggests that the act of observing a particle influences its behavior.

In essence, our consciousness actively participates in the creation of the reality we experience. The observer effect is a fascinating phenomenon in quantum physics that has profound implications for our understanding of reality. At its core, the observer effect demonstrates that the act of observing or measuring a quantum system can alter its state or behavior. In other words, the very act of observing can change the reality we are trying to study. This idea has significant implications for understanding how our thoughts and feelings influence the functioning of our bodies at a cellular and molecular level.

For example, psychoneuroimmunology examines how psychological factors, such as stress and emotions, can affect our immune system and overall health. Research in this area has shown that our thoughts and beliefs can directly influence gene expression, like adjusting the settings on a thermostat, which in turn alters cellular processes and potentially impacts our susceptibility to various health conditions. By recognizing the interconnected nature of matter, energy, and consciousness, we can better understand how our perceptions shape our health and well-being, empowering us to make more informed choices for maintaining optimal health.

To illustrate the observer effect, let's consider the famous double-slit experiment. In this experiment, scientists fire individual particles, such as electrons or photons, at a barrier with two slits. When the particles pass through the slits, they create an interference pattern on a screen behind the barrier, similar to the pattern created by waves of water passing through two openings. Interestingly, when scientists observe which slit the particle passes through, the interference pattern disappears, and the particles behave as if they were individual particles rather than waves. This change in behavior suggests that the mere act of observing the particles influences their nature, causing them to switch from wave-like behavior to particle-like behavior.

To understand this concept in simple terms, consider a real-life example involving a car's tire pressure. Imagine you want to check the tire pressure of your car. To do this, you require a tire pressure gauge. When you connect the gauge to the tire's valve stem, you allow a small amount of air to escape from the tire in order to measure the pressure. This act of observing the tire pressure inadvertently causes a slight change in the pressure itself. The tire pressure before you measured it was slightly higher than the reading you obtained from the gauge. In this example, the observer effect is demonstrated through the unavoidable change in tire pressure due to the process of measuring it. You've unintentionally altered the system by attempting to observe the system (in this case, the tire pressure). While the changes in this example may be minimal and not significantly affect the tire's performance, it illustrates the principle that observation can, in certain situations, influence the phenomenon being observed.

The observer effect has profound implications for our understanding of reality and the role of consciousness in shaping our world. It suggests that our perception and awareness can directly impact the nature of the physical world. This idea challenges the classical view of an objective, independent reality that exists outside of our observations and measurements. In a more metaphorical sense, is a powerful reminder of the interconnectedness between our thoughts, perceptions, and the world around us. Just as a painter's brushstrokes shape the canvas, our observations and perceptions shape the reality we experience. By becoming more mindful of our thoughts and intentions, we can learn to influence the world around us in more intentional and meaningful ways.

THE COMPLEXITIES OF THOUGHTS AND FEELINGS WITHIN THE BRAIN

Understanding the nature of thoughts and feelings requires delving into the complex communication system within our brains. Thoughts are electrical signals generated by neurons, the brain's primary functional units. Conversely, feelings arise from the brain's interpretation of sensory input, hormones, and neural connections. Both thoughts and feelings result from intricate interactions between neurons, which communicate through electrical impulses and chemical messengers.

Picture your thoughts and feelings as a symphony of intricate melodies, harmonies, and rhythms that arise from the complex orchestra of your brain and nervous system. Each thought is a note played by the neurons in your brain, resonating through the air and connecting with other notes to form melodies. On the other hand, feelings are like the emotional crescendos and diminuendos that give the music depth and meaning. These emotional swells result from the brain's interpretation of the sensory input from the world, interwoven with the hormones and neural connections that create a rich, emotional soundscape. Like the music of a symphony, our thoughts and feelings create an energetic composition that resonates throughout the universe. This composition, our unique electromagnetic signature, reverberates through the cosmic web, shaping the strands of our reality and influencing the interconnectedness of all things.

Neurons communicate with one another through electrical impulses called action potentials. These action potentials are generated when a neuron receives enough stimulation from other neurons, causing a shift in the balance of charged particles across the neuron's cell membrane. This shift creates a domino effect, allowing the electrical signal to propagate along the neuron's axon, a long extension that connects to other neurons. When the action potential reaches the end of the axon, it encounters a tiny gap called a synapse, which separates the neuron from its neighboring neurons. The neuron releases chemical messengers known as neurotransmitters to bridge this gap and transmit the signal. These neurotransmitters diffuse across the synapse and bind to receptors on the neighboring neuron's dendrites, specialized structures that receive incoming signals. The binding of neurotransmitters to these receptors can either excite or inhibit the receiving neuron, influencing whether it generates its own action potential.

Imagine you're at a soccer stadium, and the crowd decides to do "the wave." People stand up and sit down one after another, creating the appearance of a wave moving around the stadium. In this metaphor, each person represents a neuron, and the wave represents how neurons communicate. When a person stands up (neuron gets excited) and sits down, they're not physically moving around the stadium. Instead, the wave (communication) travels through the crowd. This is similar to how neurons communicate through excitation and de-excitation, like turning a light on and off.

Our thoughts, emotions, and behaviors arise from complex neural networks continuously transmitting chemical and electrical signals among neurons. Our brains contain billions of neurons, each forming thousands of connections with other neurons. This vast interconnected network allows for the integration of information from various brain regions, ultimately leading to the generation of conscious thought and the experience of emotions. In contrast to thoughts, our feelings are deeply intertwined with the brain's interpretation of sensory input, hormonal signals, and neural connections. Different brain regions, such as the amygdala and the insula, play essential roles in processing emotions and connecting them to our experiences. Sensory information, such as touch or smell, can evoke emotional responses by activating specific neural pathways, while hormones, such as oxytocin and cortisol, modulate our emotional states.

Being mindful of our thoughts and feelings is essential, as they directly impact our reality. We can develop greater awareness and control over our internal state through various techniques, such as meditation, journaling, and cognitive-behavioral therapy. We can improve our well-being, foster better relationships, and manifest our desires by harnessing the power of thoughts and feelings. Being intentional with our thoughts and emotions allows us to shape our electromagnetic signature, influencing the quantum field and our reality.

SHAPING OUR PERSONALITY AND OUR PERSONAL REALITY

Our personality is the lens through which we perceive and interact with the world. It influences our preferences, decisions, and reactions to different situations. In essence, our personality sets the stage for our personal reality. Our thoughts and emotions form the foundation of our personality. Throughout our lives, we develop certain thought patterns and emotional responses that become ingrained in our subconscious mind. These repetitive thoughts and emotional patterns can either support or hinder our personal growth and our ability to manifest our desires. For instance, if we continuously think negatively about ourselves, our capabilities, or our future, we will likely develop a pessimistic outlook on life. This outlook can impact our decision-making process, limit our opportunities, and hinder our ability to create the life we desire. On the other hand, cultivating positive thoughts and nurturing empowering emotional patterns can significantly enhance our personal reality. By focusing on the positive aspects of our lives and embracing a growth mindset, we can unlock our full potential and pave the way for a fulfilling and successful life.

Change begins with the conscious decision to make different choices in our thoughts, emotions, and actions. This process may involve challenging our limiting beliefs, reframing our negative thoughts, or learning new ways to manage our emotions. By recognizing our habitual thought patterns and emotional responses, we can identify areas of our personality that may hold us back. The power of choice allows us to take control of our personal reality and steer it in the direction we desire. To illustrate, consider someone who has developed a habit of thinking they are unworthy of success or happiness. To initiate change, they must first acknowledge this limiting belief and then make a conscious effort to replace it with empowering thoughts, such as "I am deserving of success and happiness." This shift in thinking can profoundly impact their personal reality and their ability to manifest their desires.

A crucial aspect of transforming our personal reality is adopting a growth mindset. This mindset is characterized by the belief that our abilities, intelligence, and potential can be developed through dedication, effort, and learning from our experiences. A growth mindset, a term coined by psychologist Carol Dweck, is a powerful approach to personal development that emphasizes the potential for growth and improvement in various aspects of our lives. It stands in contrast to a fixed mindset, characterized by the belief that our abilities, intelligence, and potential are fixed and unchangeable. A growth mindset encourages us to see challenges as opportunities to learn and grow rather than threats to our self-esteem and sense of identity.

Adopting a growth mindset nurtures an innate drive to learn and develop, as individuals recognize that their diligence and persistence can result in progress and achievement. This internal motivation propels them to strive for excellence and continuously expand their knowledge and skills. A growth mindset allows people to perceive setbacks as temporary learning opportunities rather than failures. By understanding that challenges are a natural part of growth, individuals can develop resilience and the capacity to recover from difficulties more effectively.

Embodying a growth mindset stimulates creative thinking and problem-solving abilities. With this mindset, individuals are more open to exploring unconventional strategies and approaches to tackle challenges, fostering innovation and adaptability in various situations. Cultivating a growth mindset can positively impact interpersonal relationships, as it fosters empathy, understanding, and open-mindedness. By acknowledging that others are also capable of change and growth, individuals can better appreciate diverse perspectives and experiences, leading to stronger connections with others.

Studies have shown that individuals who embrace a growth mindset report higher well-being, self-esteem, and life satisfaction. By believing in their own potential for growth and improvement, people with a growth mindset can experience a more fulfilling and rewarding life. Cultivating a growth mindset involves adopting various strategies that foster a positive and adaptive approach to personal development. It's essential to embrace challenges and seek opportunities that push you beyond your comfort zone. Challenges play a crucial role in growth and help you develop new skills while discovering your potential.

When faced with setbacks, it's important to reframe them as valuable learning experiences instead of evidence of limitations. Analyzing what went wrong and identifying areas for improvement can help you grow and make better choices in the future. Fostering a genuine curiosity and passion for learning will enable you to explore new subjects, acquire new skills, and delve deeper into your interests, contributing to your personal development.

Patience and persistence are key when pursuing growth and improvement, as real progress takes time and effort. Encourage yourself to keep pushing forward despite obstacles, knowing that each action brings you closer to your goals. Surrounding yourself with supportive individuals, such as friends, mentors, and colleagues who share a growth mindset, can provide encouragement, guidance, and constructive feedback that propels you forward.

Monitoring your self-talk is also crucial in maintaining a growth mindset. Pay attention to your internal dialogue and actively work on replacing fixed mindset thoughts with growth-oriented ones. For example, replace thoughts like "I can't do this" or "I'm not good at this" with "I can improve with practice" or "I can learn from my mistakes."

Finally, celebrate your progress and acknowledge your achievements, no matter how small they may seem. Recognizing your growth reinforces your growth mindset and motivates you to continue striving for improvement. This holistic approach to personal development enables individuals to maintain a growth mindset and experience a more fulfilling and rewarding life. By integrating these strategies into your daily life, you can foster a growth mindset that empowers you to take control of your personal reality and create the life you desire. As you embrace the potential for growth and improvement, you will unlock new possibilities and opportunities that can transform your life in meaningful and fulfilling ways.

THE CONCEPT OF THE UNKNOWN

The unknown represents a vast, multifaceted realm encompassing all aspects of existence that have not been discovered, explored, or understood. It is a vast, uncharted territory that lies beyond the boundaries of our current knowledge, experience, and perception. The unknown is ever-present and constantly evolving as new insights, discoveries, and experiences continue expanding the horizons of human understanding.

Throughout history, the concept of the unknown has captivated the human imagination and driven scientific inquiry and philosophical thought. In science, the unknown spurs researchers to develop new theories, conduct experiments, and explore previously uncharted territories in their quest for knowledge. Similarly, philosophers have grappled with the nature of the unknown, seeking to understand its implications for human existence, knowledge, and the pursuit of truth. The unknown is a realm of untapped knowledge and discovery and a space of limitless potential for personal and collective growth. By venturing into the unknown, we can uncover new talents, skills, abilities, and novel ways of thinking and interact with the world. The unknown is a treasure trove of possibilities, providing fertile ground for developing and realizing our full potential as individuals and as a species.

In our daily lives, the unknown is pervasive. It manifests in various forms, such as the uncertainty of the future, the mysteries of the human mind, and the complexities of the natural world. It is an intrinsic aspect of existence, reminding us that there will always be more to learn, explore, and understand. Embracing the unknown in everyday life enables us to remain open to new experiences, ideas, and perspectives, fostering a sense of wonder, curiosity, and humility in the face of life's infinite possibilities. From an early age, we are conditioned by society to fear the unknown. We are taught to prioritize safety, security, and predictability, often at the expense of exploration, adventure, and curiosity. This conditioning can manifest in various ways, such as an aversion to change, resistance to new ideas, and reluctance to take risks. As a result, we often develop a fear of the unknown that can hold us back from pursuing new experiences, opportunities, and growth.

Fear of the unknown can create a significant barrier to personal growth and change. It can keep us trapped in familiar patterns of thought, behavior, and emotion, stifling our potential for growth and transformation. By allowing fear to dictate our decisions and actions, we may miss out on valuable opportunities for learning, self-discovery, and manifesting our desires. One of the most powerful ways to overcome fear is to shift our perspective on the unknown. Instead of viewing the unknown as a source of potential danger or discomfort, we can see it as an opportunity for growth, learning, and self-discovery. Reframing the unknown in this way can replace fear with curiosity and excitement, empowering us to step out of our comfort zones and embrace new possibilities.

Developing resilience allows us to face the unknown with confidence, knowing that we have the inner resources and strength to cope with whatever comes our way. We can cultivate resilience by focusing on our strengths, maintaining a solid support network, and embracing a growth mindset that views challenges as opportunities for learning and growth. Taking small steps towards embracing the unknown can help us gradually build confidence and overcome fear. Instead of making significant changes or leaps, we can start by taking incremental steps towards our desired outcomes. This approach allows us to build momentum and experience small successes, which can help to reduce fear and increase our comfort with the unknown.

Overcoming fear and embracing the unknown requires cultivating trust and surrender. Trust in ourselves, our intuition, and the natural unfolding of our lives can help us let go of the need for control and predictability. Surrendering to the unknown involves releasing our attachment to specific outcomes and trusting that the universe will support us in manifesting our desires. By addressing the source of our fear, shifting our perspective, developing resilience, embracing mindfulness, taking small steps, and cultivating trust and surrender, we can overcome our fear of the unknown and harness its creative potential.

In navigating the unknown, our imagination and intuition become invaluable tools. Imagination allows us to envision new possibilities and create a mental blueprint for our desired future. Intuition, on the other hand, guides us through the unknown by offering insight and direction based on our inner wisdom and experiences. By engaging our imagination, we tap into the potential of the quantum field, aligning our thoughts and emotions with the infinite possibilities that exist within it. As we imagine new scenarios and experiences, we create an electromagnetic signature that attracts related events and circumstances into our lives. This imaginative process helps us navigate the unknown and harness the creative potential of uncertainty.

Intuition, however, is our innate ability to sense and understand information and insights that may not be immediately apparent through logic or reason. It is a valuable tool for navigating the unknown, as it can guide us towards opportunities, experiences, and decisions aligned with our desires and intentions. Developing our intuition involves cultivating a deep sense of self-awareness, trust, and openness to receiving guidance from within. Intuition is an innate sense or gut feeling that guides our decision-making process. It is a form of inner knowing that transcends logic and rational thought. Intuition often arises spontaneously and can provide valuable insights, clarity, and guidance, particularly when facing uncertainty or navigating the unknown. As we strengthen our intuition and embrace the unknown, we may experience increased synchronicities — meaningful coincidences or seemingly unrelated events that occur simultaneously or in close proximity, often leading to significant breakthroughs or realizations. These synchronicities can serve as signposts, guiding us towards opportunities and experiences that align with our desired outcomes. By paying attention to and trusting these intuitive nudges, we can more effectively navigate the uncertain terrain of the quantum field and manifest our desires.

Both imagination and intuition play essential roles in embracing the unknown and harnessing the power of uncertainty. Imagination allows us to envision new possibilities and create an electromagnetic signature aligned with our desires. At the same time, intuition helps guide us towards the experiences and opportunities that align with our intentions. By cultivating and balancing these two inner resources, we can more effectively navigate the unknown and manifest the life we desire.

QUANTUM REALITY AND CONSCIOUS CREATION

The traditional cause-and-effect model is rooted in a linear perspective, in which events and actions are viewed as occurring in sequential order. This perspective suggests that our present circumstances directly result from past events, and our current actions determine our future. This model is based on the assumption that time progresses linearly, with one event predictably leading to another. The cause-and-effect model often leads to a reactive approach to life, where we react to events and circumstances as they unfold rather than proactively shaping our future. This reactive mindset can lead to feelings of powerlessness and a belief that we have little control over the course of our lives. It can also result in a constant chase for external validation as we look to our environment and the opinions of others for a sense of worth and satisfaction.

The cause-and-effect model has several limitations. First, it assumes that events and actions can be traced back to their origins, which is only sometimes the case, especially when dealing with complex systems such as human behavior, emotions, and relationships. Second, the model focuses on observable factors and ignores the role of intangible elements, such as thoughts, emotions, and beliefs, in shaping our reality. Moreover, the cause-and-effect model discounts the possibility of multiple influences, instead promoting a one-dimensional view of how events are related. This limited perspective can result in oversimplified explanations and a narrow understanding of the many interconnected factors that shape our lives.

To break free from the limitations of the traditional cause-and-effect model, we need to shift our perspective and embrace a quantum understanding of reality. This approach acknowledges the role of thoughts, emotions, and intentions in shaping our experiences and emphasizes our innate power to create the life we desire. By adopting a quantum perspective, we can move from a reactive mindset to a proactive one, actively participating in creating our reality and embracing the limitless potential within us. The quantum model of reality is rooted in the principles of quantum mechanics, a branch of physics that explores the behavior of matter and energy at the atomic and subatomic levels. Quantum mechanics has revealed that particles, such as electrons and photons, can exist in multiple states simultaneously and that the act of observing or measuring these particles causes them to collapse into a single state, as previously mentioned with the observer effect.

Consciousness plays a crucial role in shaping our

experiences. Our thoughts, emotions, and intentions are fundamental forces interacting with the quantum field, a vast, interconnected web of energy and information permeating the entire universe. This interaction between our consciousness and the quantum field results in the manifestation of our experiences and the reality we perceive. The quantum model of reality also suggests that our universe is holographic in nature, meaning that every part of the universe contains the information for the whole. This concept is based on the idea that the fundamental building blocks of reality are not physical particles but rather patterns of information and energy.

The holographic principle implies that our reality is an interconnected web of information and that our individual experiences are reflections of the whole. The holographic principle is a fascinating concept in theoretical physics that proposes that the information contained within a particular region of space can be thought of as being encoded on a two-dimensional surface surrounding that region. In other words, it suggests that the reality we perceive as three-dimensional is actually a holographic projection of information stored on a two-dimensional surface.

To help grasp this concept, consider the analogy of a hologram on a credit card. When you look at the hologram, you see a three-dimensional image, but the information that creates the image is stored on a flat, two-dimensional surface. Similarly, our universe can be thought of as a holographic projection of information encoded on a two-dimensional surface at a deeper level of reality. This concept has profound implications for our understanding of the quantum model of reality. If our universe is indeed holographic in nature, it implies that everything is deeply and fundamentally interconnected. This interconnectivity provides a framework for understanding how our consciousness interacts with the quantum field, influencing the manifestation of our experiences and shaping our reality.

In the context of the holographic universe, our consciousness can be seen as the projector that generates the holographic reality we experience. By altering the information encoded on the two-dimensional surface (our thoughts, emotions, and intentions), we can effectively change the holographic projection (our reality). This process supports the idea that our consciousness actively participates in creating our reality, reinforcing the notion that we have the power to manifest our desired experiences. To better understand the interconnected nature of the holographic universe, imagine the universe as an infinite ocean. Each individual wave on the ocean's surface represents a separate entity or experience, but at a deeper level, all waves are connected and made of the same water. In the same way, we may perceive ourselves as separate individuals, but we are all interconnected through the quantum field that permeates the holographic universe. By recognizing this interconnectedness, we can see how our thoughts, emotions, and intentions ripple through the quantum field, influencing our experiences and shaping the reality we perceive. This understanding empowers us to take responsibility for our thoughts, emotions, and actions, ultimately allowing us to create the life we desire.

As we come to understand that our consciousness plays a crucial role in shaping our reality, we are more likely to make conscious choices that align with our desired experiences. By cultivating a clear vision of the life we want to create and maintaining a consistent focus on our intentions, we can actively participate in creating our reality and manifest the experiences we desire. Another key aspect of the quantum model of reality is the concept of nonlocality, which posits that the spatial separation between objects does not limit their ability to interact with one another. Quantum entanglement is a phenomenon that demonstrates this principle, as it shows that particles can become correlated in such a way that the state of one particle instantaneously influences the state of another, regardless of the distance between them. This interconnectedness challenges the traditional cause-and-effect model and supports the idea that our thoughts, emotions, and intentions can influence our reality beyond space and time constraints.

To help understand the concept of nonlocality and entanglement, consider the metaphor of two twins who share an extraordinary bond. Imagine that thousands of miles separate the twins, and yet, when one of them feels pain, the other instantly experiences the same sensation. This connection between the twins mirrors the relationship between entangled particles, which remain interconnected regardless of distance. This phenomenon has been famously described as "spooky action at a distance" by Albert Einstein. The nonlocality and entanglement concepts have significant implications for our understanding of consciousness and its role in the quantum model of reality. Suppose particles can be instantaneously connected regardless of the distance between them. In that case, our consciousness can also transcend space and time, influencing our reality in ways we are just beginning to understand. Quantum principles, such as nonlocality, entanglement, and the observer effect, suggest that our reality is far more interconnected and malleable than classical physics has led us to believe. These principles provide the foundation for understanding how our thoughts, emotions, and intentions can actively shape our personal experiences and create our reality.

Belief is the final piece of the puzzle in creating our reality through quantum principles. Our beliefs about ourselves, others, and the world around us shape our perception of reality, influencing our thoughts, emotions, and actions. When we believe in the power of our thoughts and emotions to shape our reality, we unlock our potential to actively participate in the creation process. By cultivating empowering beliefs and embracing the idea that we are powerful creators, we open the door to a world of limitless possibilities. To harness the power of quantum principles in our daily lives, we must consistently practice the following steps:

Set Clear Intentions for What You Want to Create or Experience

Setting clear intentions involves being specific about what you want to manifest. Write down your goals and desires, taking the time to consider why you want to achieve them and how they align with your values and purpose. This process helps solidify your intentions and provides a tangible focus point for your manifestation efforts. Regularly review and refine your intentions, staying open to the possibility of change as your life circumstances evolve, and you gain new insights.

Align Your Thoughts and Emotions With Your Intentions

To align your thoughts and emotions with your intentions, you must first become aware of your current thought patterns and emotional states. Regularly practice mindfulness and self-reflection to identify any limiting beliefs or negative emotions that may be hindering your manifestation efforts. Replace these with empowering beliefs and positive emotions by engaging in visualization, affirmations, and positive self-talk. This alignment helps to create a strong vibrational match between our inner state and the reality we desire to manifest. Cultivating positive emotions involves regularly engaging in activities that bring joy, happiness, and a sense of fulfillment. This can include spending time with loved ones, pursuing hobbies or passions, or engaging in acts of kindness and generosity. Additionally, develop a daily gratitude practice, focusing on the aspects of your life you are thankful for. These practices help maintain a high vibrational state, which is essential for attracting positive experiences and opportunities that align with your intentions. In order to cultivate empowering beliefs about yourself and your ability to shape our reality, it is essential to confront and reframe any restrictive beliefs that you might hold. Engage in regular self-reflection to identify beliefs that may be holding you back and explore their origins.

Take Inspired Action That Supports Your Intentions and Beliefs

Taking inspired action involves listening to your intuition and following through on opportunities and ideas that align with your intentions and beliefs. Trust your inner guidance and be open to the possibility that your desired reality may manifest unexpectedly. By taking consistent, inspired action, you demonstrate to the universe your commitment to manifesting your intentions and create momentum that brings your desired reality closer to fruition. Remember to celebrate your progress along the way and maintain a positive outlook, knowing you are actively co-creating your reality with the universe.

By incorporating these practices and techniques into your daily lives, you can effectively harness the power of quantum principles and create the reality you desire. The key is consistency and commitment – the more you engage with these practices, the more profound your connection to the quantum field will be.

CREATING THE FUTURE AND THE IMPORTANCE OF VISION

A compelling vision of the future is crucial to manifesting the life we desire. By creating a clear and detailed mental image of our ideal reality, we set the stage for our subconscious mind to work towards making that vision a reality. Start by considering what you truly want in life, taking into account your values, passions, and purpose. Develop a vivid picture of your future self, incorporating aspects such as career, relationships, health, and personal growth. Write down your vision and review it regularly, updating it as needed to align it with your evolving desires. To develop a truly powerful and inspiring vision, consider the following steps:

Identifying Core Values

To create a powerful and inspiring vision, it is crucial to understand your core values. These fundamental beliefs and principles guide your thoughts, actions, and decisions. Reflect on your life experiences and consider what aspects consistently resonate with you. Identifying these values will help you create an authentic, deeply-rooted vision that truly reflects your identity. Some examples of core values include integrity, family, creativity, and community.

Discovering Passions and Purpose

A compelling vision is built around your passions and purpose. Reflect on the activities, interests, and causes that truly excite you and bring a sense of meaning to your life. Identifying these elements will help you develop a vision that energizes you and keeps you motivated in the long run. Your passions and purpose may be related to your career, hobbies, social issues, or personal growth.

Setting SMART Goals

To transform your vision into actionable steps, use the SMART criteria to create goals that are Specific, Measurable, Achievable, Relevant, and Time-bound. Setting SMART goals makes your vision more tangible, allowing you to track progress, maintain focus, and stay motivated. Each goal should be a clear, concise statement outlining what you want to achieve, how you will measure success, and the timeline for completion.

Creating a Vivid Mental Image

Visualization is a powerful technique for bringing your vision to life. Spend time regularly imagining your ideal future in as much detail as possible. Consider the environment, people, feelings, and sensations associated with your vision. The more vivid and immersive your mental image, the more likely you are to manifest your desired reality.

Invoking Positive Emotions

Positive emotions are crucial in manifesting your vision. As you visualize your ideal future, focus on the emotions you would experience, such as joy, gratitude, and love. These emotions create a positive feedback loop, reinforcing your vision and attracting the desired experiences and outcomes.

Writing It Down

Documenting your vision in writing is essential in solidifying it. Use descriptive language to capture the essence of what you want to create or experience. This written record serves as a tangible reminder of your vision and provides a reference for tracking progress, celebrating achievements, and making adjustments as needed.

Reviewing and Revising Regularly

Your vision is a dynamic, evolving construct that should be regularly revisited and updated. As you grow and change, your desires, priorities, and circumstances may shift. Regularly reviewing and revising your vision ensures it remains relevant and aligned with your current values, passions, and goals. Set aside time to reflect on your vision, assess progress, and make necessary adjustments to keep it fresh and inspiring. By developing a compelling vision that is deeply rooted in your values, passions, and purpose, you set the stage for a powerful manifestation process that can transform your reality and bring your dreams to life. To live fully in the present, you must first overcome the limiting beliefs that hold you back. Emotional attachments, whether to past experiences, certain outcomes, or other people, can impede your ability to manifest your desired future. In order to move forward, it's crucial to release these attachments and free yourself from the constraints they impose. The following steps can help you release emotional attachments and enable your personal growth:

Recognizing the Attachment

The process of releasing emotional attachments begins with self-awareness. Reflect on the aspects of your life where you feel stagnant or unable to progress and identify any emotions or situations that seem to hold you back. By acknowledging the existence of these attachments, you can begin to understand their impact on your life and take steps towards releasing them.

Understanding the Root Cause

To effectively release emotional attachments, it's important to explore their underlying reasons. Emotional attachments often stem from unmet needs, fears, or insecurities that may have originated in past experiences or relationships. By delving into the reasons for your attachments, you can begin to confront and resolve the deeper issues at play, making it easier to let go of the emotions or situations keeping you stuck.

Practicing Self-Compassion

Releasing emotional attachments requires a compassionate and non-judgmental approach. Recognize that forming attachments is a natural human response and that experiencing the associated emotions is part of the healing process. Validate your feelings and remind yourself that letting go of attachments is a journey of self-discovery, personal growth, and emotional healing.

Letting Go of Control

One key aspect of releasing emotional attachments is accepting that you cannot control everything. Embrace the inherent uncertainty in life, and understand that situations may not always unfold as you envision. Trust that letting go of these attachments creates space for new opportunities, experiences, and personal growth. Cultivate an attitude of surrender and openness to the possibilities that lie ahead.

Fostering New Connections

As you work to release emotional attachments, actively seek out new experiences and relationships that align with your values and desired future. Engage in activities that bring joy, satisfaction, and personal growth, and surround yourself with a supportive network of individuals who uplift and inspire you. By fostering new connections and immersing yourself in positive experiences, you can gradually replace old attachments with healthier, more fulfilling bonds that promote growth.

By following these steps, you can release emotional attachments and empower yourself to embrace the future with confidence and a renewed sense of purpose. As you let go of the past and the constraints that have held you back, you'll be better equipped to manifest the life you desire. Embodying greatness involves adopting the mindset, habits, and behaviors of those who have succeeded in their chosen fields. Cultivate these qualities within yourself through daily practice, and strive to continually improve and grow as you work towards your goals:

Studying Inspiring Individuals

Begin your journey towards greatness by learning from those who have achieved it. Examine the lives and works of people who inspire you, and identify the qualities that contributed to their success. These qualities may include resilience, courage, creativity, empathy, or adaptability. Your definition of greatness should be unique to you, reflecting your values and aspirations and serving as a guiding light on your path.

Cultivating Self-Awareness

Developing self-awareness is crucial in understanding how you can embody greatness. Engage in regular reflection and introspection to identify areas where you can improve or adopt the qualities associated with greatness. Assess your strengths and weaknesses, and seek feedback from others to gain a well-rounded understanding of your progress and areas for growth.

Breaking Down Greatness Into Smaller Goals

To maintain focus and momentum on your path to greatness, break your larger vision into smaller, achievable goals. These goals provide a roadmap for your journey and offer a sense of accomplishment as you make progress towards your larger objectives.

Fostering a Growth Mindset

Embrace a mindset that views challenges as opportunities, learns from failure, and sees setbacks as chances for growth. This mindset will enable you to continuously evolve, adapt to new situations, and propel yourself towards greatness.

Establishing Supportive Routines and Practices

Create daily routines and practices that align with your vision of greatness. This may involve engaging in regular exercise, maintaining a healthy diet, practicing meditation or mindfulness, or seeking out new learning opportunities. These routines and practices will help you build a strong foundation for your journey towards greatness.

Consistent Action and Dedication

Achieving greatness requires ongoing commitment and dedication to your vision. Prioritize actions that align with your goals, and stay focused on the steps needed to embody greatness. Celebrate your successes along the way, using your accomplishments as fuel to propel you forward and stay motivated on your journey.

As you cultivate the qualities and habits associated with greatness, you'll naturally attract opportunities and experiences that support your vision and bring you closer to your goals to create lasting change. Change is an inevitable part of life and a driving force behind personal growth and evolution. Embrace change as an opportunity to learn, grow, and transform your reality. Develop resilience and adaptability by viewing change as a natural, essential component of the manifestation process. Trust that each new experience brings you closer to realizing your vision of the future.

Change challenges us to reassess our beliefs, habits, and attitudes and enables us to adapt to new circumstances and environments. Change often reveals hidden strengths, talents, and passions that may have been dormant or overlooked. We gain a deeper understanding of ourselves and uncover new facets of our identity, ultimately leading to greater self-awareness and personal growth. Change sparks creativity, encouraging us to think outside the box, explore new ideas, and find innovative solutions to problems. It can also serve as a catalyst for forging deeper connections with others. We can build stronger, more meaningful relationships based on shared experiences, empathy, and mutual support by navigating change together. We can better evolve and develop as individuals by confronting our fears, pushing our boundaries, and embracing new experiences. Change exposes us to new ideas, cultures, and perspectives that can enrich our lives and broaden our worldview. As we embrace change, we become more open-minded and receptive to the diverse array of possibilities that life has to offer. We can transform our lives, overcome limitations, and unlock our full potential by harnessing the power of change.

CONCLUSION

As we approach the end of this transformative journey together and prepare to close the final chapter of this book, it is important to pause, reflect, and appreciate the progress we have made thus far. Throughout these pages, we have delved deep into the mysteries of the human mind, exploring its intricacies and learning to harness its extraordinary power. Now, as we stand on the height of newfound understanding and personal growth, let us take a moment to acknowledge the insights we have gained and the lessons we have learned, for they will serve as the foundation upon which we continue to build our lives and reach our full potential.

May this book serve as a stepping stone, providing you with the knowledge, strategies, and insights necessary to embark on this transformative path. As you continue to explore and apply the wisdom shared throughout these pages, you will find yourself better equipped to navigate life's challenges and opportunities. We have explored the intricacies of the human mind, the power of habits, the influence of epigenetics, the potential of neuroplasticity, the placebo effect, the science behind brainwaves and meditation, the importance of coherence, and the fascinating realm of quantum reality. These diverse concepts and teachings are interconnected, culminating in the understanding that you hold the key within you to unlock your full potential and master your mind.

Remember that self-discovery is a dynamic and evolving process. As you continue to learn, grow, and evolve, you will inevitably encounter new doors waiting to be opened, each revealing a deeper understanding of your true self. Embrace these opportunities, and let them guide you towards a more purposeful, fulfilling, and empowered life. As you progress on this journey, it is essential to maintain an open mind and a growth-oriented mindset. Be willing to challenge your beliefs, question your assumptions, and embrace new perspectives. Doing so will uncover hidden strengths, develop new skills, and expand your horizons, allowing you to redefine and refine your sense of self continually.

Furthermore, it is vital to cultivate self-compassion and patience as you traverse this winding path of personal growth. In its inherent complexity, life is a continuous ebb and flow of triumphs and challenges. To truly understand this journey, consider the metaphor of bicycle pedals. Just as the pedals need to move both up and down to propel the bicycle forward, we must also experience the highs and lows to progress in our lives. Embrace the wisdom gained from your successes and setbacks, and recognize that each of these experiences serves a unique purpose in shaping your overall journey. It is within this duality of life that we learn our most profound lessons and develop the necessary resilience, adaptability, and inner fortitude to navigate the ever-changing landscape of our existence.

As you continue on this path, remember that every challenge you face provides an opportunity for growth. Treat these moments with the same kindness and patience as you would your victories, for they are equally important in guiding you towards your ultimate destination. Maintaining an open heart and mind and embracing life's inherent ups and downs will foster a deeper connection with yourself and cultivate the resilience required to keep moving forward. In doing so, you will progress on your journey and inspire others to embark on their own paths towards self-actualization and growth.

As you continue to explore your inner landscape and uncover the many facets of your true self, you will also discover the interconnectedness of all things. Recognize the impact you have on the world around you and the profound influence others have on your life. By cultivating a sense of responsibility, empathy, and compassion towards others, you will not only enrich your own life but also contribute to the betterment of the world around you. Free will is a powerful force that allows you to choose how you converse with the world and shape your experiences. Your choices, actions, and experiences lead to growth, giving rise to wisdom. This wisdom encompasses all the teachings presented in this book, providing you with the knowledge and tools to navigate life with clarity, purpose, and intention. Each of us already possesses everything we need to embark on the journey of self-discovery and create positive transformation in our lives. The innate wisdom, strength, and resilience within us are like hidden treasures, waiting to be uncovered and harnessed as we navigate the complexities of existence.

In this interconnected world, let your journey inspire others. Share your experiences, insights, and lessons learned, and encourage those around you to embark on their own transformative paths. By fostering a community of growth, support, and empowerment, you will help to create a world filled with purpose, passion, and boundless potential. Consider the metaphor of a seed. Within each tiny seed lies the potential to grow into a magnificent tree. The seed already contains all the genetic information necessary to become a towering, fruitful entity. It simply needs the right conditions—nourishment, sunlight, and water—to unleash its inherent potential. Similarly, we hold within ourselves the raw ingredients for growth and transformation. Our mission is to create the right environment and conditions to allow our inner potential to flourish.

As the author, my role has been to guide you through the portal of self-discovery and transformation, unveiling the possibilities that lie within your reach. However, the ultimate responsibility of walking through this portal and embracing your potential rests with you. Your choices, courage, and commitment will determine the course of your life and the realization of your dreams. The knowledge presented within the pages of this book is the culmination of years of research, reflection, conversations, seminars, studies and experiences, all woven together by the hands of a fellow human being in pursuit of understanding our collective and individual purpose and existence in the present moment. It is important to acknowledge that we may never fully comprehend the intricacies and complexities of this vast universe or the nature of our reality. However, the relentless pursuit of truth and understanding fuels our passion for life and drives us to continually seek new experiences and insights.

If this book has inspired even one person to embark on their journey of self-discovery, growth, and personal transformation, it has undoubtedly fulfilled its purpose. The ideas and concepts presented within these pages may not resonate with everyone initially, as our perceptions and focus are shaped by our unique experiences and current state of mind. For those who cannot fully grasp the concepts or ideas presented, I encourage you to revisit this book at different points in your life, as your evolving perspective may reveal new layers of understanding and meaning.

As time passes, more individuals are stepping forward to contribute their discoveries and insights about the human mind, body, and our connection to the universe. Each new piece of information adds to our collective understanding, gradually revealing a clearer picture of our existence within this plane. This book is a tribute to all those who have dedicated their lives to unraveling the mysteries of our existence and who have, through their tireless efforts, illuminated the path for others to follow. In the spirit of never-ending growth, learning, and self-improvement, let us always remember to honor and value our unique existence. Each of us is an integral part of this reality, and our presence is just as valuable and significant as anyone else's. The universe would not be the same without each of us, and it is our shared responsibility to contribute to the greater good by striving to reach our full potential and helping others do the same.

As you close the pages of this book and move forward in your life, may you be inspired to continue your journey. Embrace your unique place in the universe, and cherish the opportunities that lie before you. Continue seeking out new experiences and knowledge, and never stop pursuing your passion for truth, understanding, and self-discovery. Let this book serve as a reminder to live a life of constant introspection, growth, and self-improvement, for it is through this journey that we uncover the true essence of our existence and come to appreciate the infinite potential that resides within each and every one of us. With gratitude and respect for all who have contributed to this body of work, let us forge ahead, united in our quest for knowledge, understanding, and the realization of our full potential. Together, we can elevate the human experience and bring light to the darkness, creating a better world for ourselves and future generations.

Lastly, always remember that the journey of self-discovery is unique to each individual. Embrace your path, and honor the experiences and wisdom that have shaped your life thus far. As you continue to grow, evolve, and find your place in this world, know that you possess the power to create a life that truly reflects your passions, values, and dreams. Let this book be a catalyst for change, a beacon of hope, and a constant reminder of your limitless potential. May the knowledge, insights, and wisdom shared throughout these pages guide your journey towards self-discovery, personal growth, and a deeper understanding of your true self. Here's to a future filled with endless possibilities, unshakable inner strength, and the unwavering conviction that you are capable of achieving your greatest dreams. Enjoy the journey, trust in your potential, and boldly step forward into the life you were always meant to live. In the words of the ancient philosopher Lao Tzu,

"Knowing others is intelligence; knowing yourself is true wisdom. Mastering others is strength; mastering yourself is true power."

Mastering the free mind is an odyssey of transcending the self-imposed boundaries of thought, liberating our consciousness to dwell in the infinite realm of wisdom and possibility.

With love,
Gabriel O. Daniels

GUIDED MEDITATION

Meditation can be a highly individual practice, and finding a method that resonates with you is essential. This guide aims to provide a framework that you can follow and adjust according to your needs:

Find a quiet and comfortable place where you won't be disturbed. Sit down with your back straight and your hands resting on your lap.

Close your eyes and take a few deep breaths, inhaling through your nose and exhaling through your mouth. Feel the air entering and leaving your body, and allow yourself to relax.

Bring your attention to the present moment. Notice any sounds around you, the temperature of the air, and the sensation of your body on the chair or cushion.

Begin to focus on your breath, taking deep, slow breaths in and out through your nose. As you breathe in, imagine drawing in positive energy; as you breathe out, release any negative energy.

With each breath, allow your mind to slow down and let go of any thoughts or distractions. You might find it helpful to visualize each thought as a cloud passing by or a leaf floating down a stream.

As you continue breathing, you may become more aware of the chatter in your conscious mind. Notice these thoughts without judgment and let them pass by like clouds in the sky.

Now, bring your attention to your body. Starting from your toes, slowly scan your body with your mind, noticing any areas of tension or discomfort. As you breathe in, imagine sending healing energy to these areas, and as you breathe out, release the tension. Take as much time as you need to scan your body.

As you continue to scan your body, you may become aware of automatic thoughts or behaviors that are often influenced by your subconscious mind. Notice these thoughts without judgment and simply observe them as they pass by.

Continue to meditate, observing your thoughts and allowing them to pass by until you feel ready to end your practice.

As you come to an end, take a few deep breaths and slowly bring your attention back to the present moment. When you're ready, gently open your eyes.

Regular practice will make you more attuned to your body and mind, allowing you to deepen your meditation practice and explore new dimensions of consciousness. So don't be discouraged if you don't experience immediate results; keep practicing, and you'll find that your meditations become more meaningful and transformative over time. Remember, the journey towards greater self-awareness and inner peace is a lifelong process, so embrace it with an open heart and mind and enjoy meditation's many benefits.

The transformative power of meditation lies in its ability to help us access and work with the hidden realms of our subconscious mind. By consistently practicing meditation, we can gain insight into our automatic thoughts, beliefs, and habits and transform them to create a more empowered and authentic version of ourselves. Establishing a consistent meditation practice requires patience and perseverance, but the rewards are well worth the effort. As we continue to explore the science and practice of meditation, we open ourselves to the limitless potential for growth, healing, and self-discovery within each of us.

CITATION

4edges. (2018, October 24). Plato's Allegory of the Cave [Digital image]. Retrieved from https://commons.wikimedia.org/wiki/File:An_Illustration_of_The_Allegory_of_the_Cave,_from_Plato%E2%80%99s_Republic.jpg

Beecher, H. K. (1946). Pain in men wounded in battle. Annals of Surgery, 123(3), 96-105. doi:10.1097/00000658-194603000-00007

Benedetti, F., Pollo, A., Lopiano, L., Lanotte, M., Vighetti, S., & Rainero, I. (2003). Conscious expectation and unconscious conditioning in analgesic, motor, and hormonal placebo/nocebo responses. Journal of Neuroscience, 23(10), 4315-4323. doi: 10.1523/JNEUROSCI.23-10-04315.2003.

Black, D. S., & Slavich, G. M. (2016). Mindfulness meditation and the immune system: a systematic review of randomized controlled trials. Annals of the New York Academy of Sciences, 1373(1), 13-24. https://doi.org/10.1111/nyas.12998

Black, D. S., Cole, S. W., Irwin, M. R., Breen, E., St. Cyr, N. M., & Nazarian, N. (2016). Alterations in brain and immune function produced by mindfulness meditation. Psychiatry Research, 251, 65-71. https://doi.org/10.1016/j.psychres.2016.12.052

Boks, M. P., van Mierlo, H. C., Rutten, B. P., & Kas, M. J. (2019). Epigenetic mechanisms in anxiety and stress-related disorders Progress in molecular biology and translational science, 157, 285-305. doi: 10.1016/bs.pmbts.2018.12.007

Byrd, R. C., & Clayton, R. H. (1984). The psychoneuroimmunology of placebo effects: Historical and conceptual review. In A. A. Baum & J. E. Singer (Eds.), Handbook of psychology and health (Vol. 4, pp. 67-100). Hillsdale, NJ: Erlbaum.

Chopra, D. (2018). The healing self: A revolutionary new plan to supercharge your immunity and stay well for life. Random House.

Dias, B. G., & Ressler, K. J. (2014). Parental olfactory experience influences behavior and neural structure in subsequent generations. Nature neuroscience, 17(1), 89-96.

Edgar Cayce's Association for Research and Enlightenment. (2022). About Edgar Cayce. https://www.edgarcayce.org/edgar-cayce/his-life/

Emmons, R. A., & Stern, R. (2013). Gratitude as a psychotherapeutic intervention. Journal of Clinical Psychology, 69(8), 846-855. https://doi.org/10.1002/jclp.22020

Finniss, D. G., Kaptchuk, T. J., Miller, F., & Benedetti, F. (2010). Biological, clinical, and ethical advances of placebo effects. The Lancet, 375(9715), 686-695. doi: 10.1016/s0140-6736(09)61706-2

Francis, D. D., Meaney, M. J., & Szyf, M. (1999). Maternal care, gene expression, and the transmission of individual differences in stress reactivity across generations. Annals of the New York Academy of Sciences, 896(1), 66-84. doi:10.1111/j.1749-6632.1999.tb08103.x

Frewen, P. A., Evans, E. M., Maraj, N., Dozois, D. J. A., & Partridge, K. (2018). Letting go: Mindfulness and negative automatic thinking. Cognitive Therapy and Research, 42(3), 341-352. https://contextualscience.org/system/files/Frewen,2008.pdf SEP

Gupta, S. (2018). The Science of Neuroplasticity and How to Rewire Your Brain. Harvard Business Review. https://hbr.org/2018/05/the-science-of-neuroplasticity-and-how-to-rewire-your-brain SEP

Harvard Health Publishing. (2018, February). How emotions can affect genetic expression. https://developingchild.harvard.edu/resources/early-experiences-can-alter-gene-expression-and-affect-long-term-development/ SEP

Hildegard of Bingen. (n.d.). The official website of the Hildegard von Bingen Foundation. https://hildegardvonbingen.org/hildegard-life/ SEP

Hölzel, B. K., Carmody, J., Evans, K. C., Hoge, E. A., Dusek, J. A., Morgan, L., ... & Lazar, S. W. (2010). Mindfulness practice leads to increases in regional brain gray matter density. Psychiatry Research: Neuroimaging, 191(1), 36-43. https://doi.org/10.1016/j.pscychresns.2010.08.006

Hölzel, B. K., Carmody, J., Vangel, M., Congleton, C., Yerramsetti, S. M., Gard, T., & Lazar, S. W. (2011). Mindfulness practice leads to increases in regional brain gray matter density. Psychiatry Research: Neuroimaging, 191(1), 36-43. doi: 10.1016/j.pscychresns.2010.08.006

Kaptchuk, T. J., & Miller, F. G. (2015). Placebo effects in medicine. New England Journal of Medicine, 373(1), 8-9. doi: 10.1056/NEJMc1504023

Kiecolt-Glaser, J. K., McGuire, L., Robles, T. F., & Glaser, R. (2002). Psychoneuroimmunology: Psychological influences on immune function and health. Journal of Consulting and Clinical Psychology, 70(3), 537–547. https://doi.org/10.1037/0022-006x.70.3.537

Kini, P., Wong, J., McInnis, S., Gabana, N., & Brown, J. W. (2016). The effects of gratitude expression on neural activity. NeuroImage, 128, 1-10. doi: 10.1016/j.neuroimage.2015.12.040

Kyeong, S., Kim, J. E., & Kim, J. (2017). Effects of gratitude meditation on neural network functional connectivity and brain-heart coupling. Psychiatry Research: Neuroimaging, 269, 1-7. doi: 10.1016/j.pscychresns.2017.09.007

Lipton, B. H. (2005). The biology of belief: Unleashing the power of consciousness, matter & miracles. Hay House, Inc.

Lin, I.-M., Okazaki, Y. O., & Brimmer, D. J. (2019). Mind-body interconnectivity: Gamma brainwave and the influence of positive emotions. Cognitive and Behavioral Neurology, 32(4), 247-251. https://pubmed.ncbi.nlm.nih.gov/14678580/

Lyon, D. E., Jackson, J. J., & Schapiro, N. A. (2020). Epigenetics and collective trauma: implications for social justice and health equity. Journal of Human Rights and Social Work, 5(4), 289-298. https://doi.org/10.1007/s41134-020-00157-9

McCraty, R., Atkinson, M., Tiller, W. A., Rein, G., & Watkins, A. D. (1995). The effects of emotions on short-term power spectrum analysis of heart rate variability. American Journal of Cardiology, 76(14), 1089-1093.

McGowan, P. O., Sasaki, A., D'Alessio, A. C., Dymov, S., Labonté, B., Szyf, M., ... Meaney, M. J. (2009). Epigenetic regulation of the glucocorticoid receptor in human brain associates with childhood abuse. Nature Neuroscience, 12(3), 342-348. doi:10.1038/nn.2270

McEwen, B. S. (2008). Central effects of stress hormones in health and disease: Understanding the protective and damaging effects of stress and stress mediators. European Journal of Pharmacology, 583(2-3), 174-185. https://doi.org/10.1016/j.ejphar.2007.11.071

McLynn, F. (1996). Carl Gustav Jung: A biography. St. Martin's Press.

McNab, F., & Klingberg, T. (2008). Prefrontal cortex and basal ganglia control access to working memory. Nature neuroscience, 11(1), 103-107. doi: 10.1038/nn2024

Mehdizadeh, S., & Abassi, M. (2021). The effectiveness of biofeedback therapy on depression, anxiety and stress in patients with major depressive disorder: A randomized controlled trial. Journal of Psychiatric Research, 141, 96-103. doi: 10.1016/j.jpsychires.2021.04.050

Melamed, S., Ugarten, U., Shirom, A., Kahana, L., Lerman, Y., & Froom, P. (1999). Chronic burnout, somatic arousal and elevated salivary cortisol levels. Journal of Psychosomatic Research, 46(6), 591-598. https://doi.org/10.1016/s0022-3999(99)00090-8

Nestoriuc, Y., Rief, W., & Martin, A. (2008). Meta-analysis of biofeedback for tension-type headache: efficacy, specificity, and treatment moderators. Journal of Headache and Pain, 9(4), 197-209. doi: 10.1007/s10194-008-0054-6

Nouchi, R., Taki, Y., Takeuchi, H., Hashizume, H., Akitsuki, Y., Shigemune, Y., ... & Kawashima, R. (2013). Brain training game improves executive functions and processing speed in the elderly: a randomized controlled trial. PloS one, 8(3), e5856. https://pubmed.ncbi.nlm.nih.gov/22253758/

[⊥SEP]Peat, F. D. (1997). Infinite potential: The life and times of David Bohm. Addison-Wesley.

[⊥SEP]Petrovic, P., Kalso, E., Petersson, K. M., & Ingvar, M. (2002). Placebo and opioid analgesia— imaging a shared neuronal network. Science, 295(5560), 1737-1740. doi: 10.1126/science.1067176.

Price, D. D., Finniss, D. G., & Benedetti, F. (2008). A comprehensive review of the placebo effect: Recent advances and current thought. Annual Review of Psychology, 59, 565-590. doi:10.1146/annurev.psych.59.103006.093629

Radtke, K. M., Ruf, M., Gunter, H. M., Dohrmann, K., Schauer, M., Meyer, A., ... & Elbert, T. (2011). Transgenerational impact of intimate partner violence on methylation in the promoter of the glucocorticoid receptor. Translational psychiatry, 1(7), e21. https://doi.org/10.1038/tp.2011.21

Rollin, G., & Leduc, A. (2020). The heart and the brain: Coherence as a key to effective psychotherapy. Journal of Psychotherapy Integration, 30(3), 361-377. https://doi.org/10.1037/int0000216

Rollin McCraty, Ph.D., Mike Atkinson, and Raymond Trevor Bradley, "Electrophysiological Evidence of Intuition: Part 2. A System-Wide Process?," Journal of Alternative and Complementary Medicine 10, no. 2 (2004): 325-336.

Segerstrom, S. C., & Miller, G. E. (2004). Psychological Stress and the Human Immune System: A Meta-Analytic Study of 30 Years of Inquiry. Psychological Bulletin, 130(4), 601–630. https://doi.org/10.1037/0033-2909.130.4.601

Schutte, N. S., Malouff, J. M., Hall, L. E., Haggerty, D. J., Cooper, J. T., Golden, C. J., & Dornheim, L. (2014). Development and validation of a measure of emotional intelligence. Personality and Individual Differences, 65, 53-57. doi: 10.1016/j.paid.2014.01.004

Sheldrake, R. (1981). A new science of life: The hypothesis of formative causation. Blond & Briggs.

Sheldrake, R. (2012). Science set free: 10 paths to new discovery. Deepak Chopra Books. Sheldrake, R. (1988). The presence of the past: Morphic resonance and the habits of nature. Times Books.

Szyf, M., Weaver, I. C. G., & Meaney, M. J. (2007). The social environment and the epigenome. Environmental and Molecular Mutagenesis, 48(1), 46-60. doi:10.1002/em.20237

Tang, Y.-Y., Lu, Q., Fan, M., Yang, Y., & Posner, M. I. (2012). Mechanisms of white matter changes induced by meditation. Proceedings of the National Academy of Sciences, 109(26), 10570-10574. https://doi.org/10.1073/pnas.1207817109

Tang, Y. Y., Lu, Q., Geng, X., Stein, E. A., Yang, Y., & Posner, M. I. (2010). Short-term meditation induces white matter changes in the anterior cingulate. Proceedings of the National Academy of Sciences, 107(35), 15649-15652. doi: 10.1073/pnas.1011043107

Tesla Universe. (n.d.). Nikola Tesla: The inventor. https://teslauniverse.com/nikola-tesla

The Nobel Prize. (n.d.). Albert Einstein - Biographical.
https://www.nobelprize.org/prizes/physics/1921/einstein/biographical/

Valenzuela, M. J., & Sachdev, P. (2006). Brain reserve and dementia: a systematic review. Psychological medicine, 36(4), 441-454. doi: 10.1017/S0033291705006264

Vestergaard-Poulsen, P., van Beek, M., Skewes, J., Bjarkam, C. R., Stubberup, M., Bertelsen, J., & Roepstorff, A. (2009). Long-term meditation is associated with increased gray matter density in the brain stem. Frontiers in Human Neuroscience, 3, 1-9. doi: 10.3389/neuro.09.015.2009

Weaver, I. C. G., Cervoni, N., Champagne, F. A., D'Alessio, A. C., Sharma, S., Seckl, J. R., … Meaney, M. J. (2004). Epigenetic programming by maternal behavior. Nature Neuroscience, 7(8), 847-854. doi:10.1038/nn1276

Wheeler, J. A. (1999). Geometrodynamics and the issue of the final state. Annals of the New York Academy of Sciences, 896(1), 1-14. doi: 10.1111/j.1749-6632.1999.tb08134.x

Yeager, D. S., & Dweck, C. S. (2018). Mindsets that promote resilience: When students believe that personal characteristics can be developed. Educational Psychologist, 53(2), 110-120.
https://www.researchgate.net/publication/262908828_Mindsets_That_Promote_Resilienc e_When_Students_Believe_That_Personal_Characteristics_Can_Be_Developed

Printed in Great Britain
by Amazon

34402193R00169